"a poor, damn'd, rascally Gager

Robert Burns the Exciseman

© GRAHAM SMITH

First Published in 1989
by
Alloway Publishing Ltd.,
Ayr.

Printed in Scotland
by
Walker & Connell Ltd.,
Hastings Square, Darvel,
Ayrshire.

ISBN 0-907526-43-8

"a poor, damn'd, rascally Gager"

Robert Burns the Exciseman

Graham Smith

Alloway Publishing
AYR

INDEX OF ILLUSTRATIONS

Page references printed after quotations refer to the page where the full text of either the poem or letter may be found in Alloway Publishing's editions of *The Complete Works of Robert Burns* or *The Complete Letters of Robert Burns.*

FOREWORD

by Sir Angus Fraser,
Chairman of the Board
of
HM Customs & Excise,
1983 – 87

There have been many popular misconceptions about Burns's life, not least about his career as an Exciseman. It is good that Graham Smith has been able to set the Excise record straight in this book.

The literary world of the day appeared to think that it was a dishonour for Scotland's Bard to be a gauger. Burns himself had mixed feelings. Lately he had been the toast of Edinburgh and had known wide acclaim and been welcomed at the tables of the gentry. But he refused to let his meteoric rise to fame go to his head and was painfully aware of the lack of security for himself and his ever-growing family in continuing as a poor tenant-farmer. If nothing else, there was in the Excise no loss of income because of bad land, or a bad harvest, or bad weather. And so, for the last seven years of his life, Burns gave himself seriously and conscientiously to a service that was more efficient and honourable than many other branches of government at that time. In some ways it meant that he had to be more circumspect than before in expressing himself, as he found to his humiliation when he was forced to recant after displaying sympathy with the French Revolution; but his contemporaries were mistaken in thinking that the Excise would inhibit his poetic output. That he succeeded in writing poems of the calibre of *Tam o' Shanter* and the songs which were the consuming interest of his last years are ample proof that his creative genius was never higher.

Burns enjoyed the respect and goodwill of his Excise colleagues and made some good friends there. Later members of the Department–now the combined Department of Customs and Excise–have continued to take pride in the association. The departmental Museum is not short of literary relics, but Burns memorabilia have always been well to the fore–most notably the 'character book' which refers to him as *'The Poet, does pretty well.'* When the tercentenary of the English Excise was being celebrated in 1983, the fact that it was the English Excise was not allowed to exclude Burns from a prominent place in the specially mounted exhibition. I have no doubt that when the tercentenary of the Scottish Excise is in turn celebrated in the year 2007, the occasion will lend further support to Gladstone's dictum of 1895: *'The loyalty of the Excise to the Poet is very remarkable and does credit to both'.*

PORTRAIT OF BURNS WITH EXTRACT OF HIS WORK AS
ACTING SUPERVISOR. *(HMSO)*.

Chapter One

The *'poor, damn'd, rascally Gager'*, as Robert Burns described himself (C.L.p.315), has become the most famous Exciseman of all time. He once expressed the earnest hope that his profession should borrow credit from him and this wish has been fully realised well beyond his wildest dreams. It is almost two hundred years since the poet entered the Scottish Excise service and yet Her Majesty's Customs and Excise still take an immense pride in perhaps its most celebrated officer.

Robert Burns, like so many writers before and after him, was forced to seek a secure but somewhat meagre living in the Government service to help support his literary work. But his renown as a tax collector places him above such other distinguished literary figures as Ashmole, Allingham, Chaucer, Congreve, Defoe, Dryden, Galt, Paine, Adam Smith, Trollope and Wordsworth—all of whom held positions in the revenue services at some time during their lives. It is not universally known for instance that Chaucer was a Customs Comptroller in London or indeed that Wordsworth was a Distributor for Stamp duties in Westmorland; but Burns is pre-eminently known as the poet AND Exciseman. Despite this fact and considering the wealth of published material on all aspects of his life, it is surprising how very little has been written about his life as an Excise officer.

The last seven years of his all too brief life was spent in the service of the Scottish Excise, and it was during this period that he produced some of his finest poems—*Tam o' Shanter* is a notable example. He also worked tirelessly and assiduously on the collections of songs as well as maintaining a prolific and lively correspondence. All this was undertaken whilst still attending to his full and, at times, arduous Excise duties, which occupied him with numerous visits during the day and with books and accounts late into the night. That this punishing work-load was also attended by increasing ill-health makes Burns's achievements in his latter years even more remarkable. The diligence, energy and enthusiasm that he gave not only to his various literary endeavours but also to his official duties were really quite amazing. One writer on Burns has recently suggested that his Excise post was a sinecure. Not only is that manifestly incorrect, but such a statement does a grave disservice to the considerable achievements of the poet and revenue officer.

The Excise in England and Scotland was a much maligned service and its officers were universally loathed and despised. Dr. Johnson's opinion expressed in his dictionary, first published in 1755, was quite normal for the age. He defined

'Excise' as, '*a hateful tax levied upon commodities and adjudged not by the common judges of property but by wretches hired by those to whom the excise is paid.*' Certainly Burns harboured no illusions as to the popularity of the Service he had entered. He quite obviously felt the need to try to explain to his friends his reasons for taking such a momentous step because many of his letters are larded with apologies for his decision.

On the face of it Burns would seem to be a most unlikely candidate for service in the Excise. His strong revolutionary sympathies appear to be at direct variance to the holding of any Government post under George III. Also his ardent and staunch nationalistic feelings would seem quite contrary to employment in the Scottish Excise, which for many Scots was the omnipresent reminder of the detested Act of Union. Furthermore Burns had always abhorred those minor officials who stood between the rich and the poor and greatly abused their power; and yet he joined their very ranks and found himself, '*grinding the faces of the Publican and the Sinner on the merciless wheels of the Excise*' (C.L.p.465). Thus it is surprising to find Burns as an Excise officer and then to discover that he made an unqualified success of the job is, perhaps, even more remarkable.

Burns wrote of '*the ignominy of the Excise*' (C.L.p.339 and 498), and in this he was merely expressing the widely accepted view of the tax. Indeed most people, both in England and Scotland, considered the dreaded Excise as the most fiendish and detestable duty ever devised by man. However, it must be remembered that it was not until 1799 that income tax made its first unwelcome entry into the taxation field to rival or even surpass the Excise in unpopularity! But why had the Excise incurred such odium?

Several forms of Excise duty had been in existence on the Continent in the early years of the seventeenth century and perhaps the most successful of them was in operation in the United Netherlands; it was known as 'accius' and the word 'excise' may be a corruption of the Dutch. In 1626 Charles I had attempted to introduce a general Excise based on the Netherlands model but such was the intensity of popular opposition to the proposal that Parliament turned it down flat. It was considered '*a foreign monster that would devour the nation*'! And yet, less than twenty years later, Parliament itself was forced to resort to this '*hated foreign monster*'.

The first Excise duty was introduced into England and Wales on 22nd July 1643. The avowed intention of this new and quite radical tax was to raise money to finance the Parliamentary army in its long and bitter struggle against Charles I. The duty was first imposed for one year only and when it came up for renewal it was merely extended for the duration of the war. Like most '*temporary*' taxes, however, it quickly acquired the bad habit of permanence and now, over three hundred years later, Excise duties form a very substantial part of the revenue of the United Kingdom.

The Excise was basically a duty charged on home-produced goods, unlike the Customs duties, which are levied on imported goods. In the first instance the duty fell on ale and beer, strong waters (spirits) and cider, but all too soon it was extended to other goods and even included some imported goods. Year by year the goods liable to duty grew and grew, thus confirming the worst fears of its opponents, that an Excise lends itself easily to a general and wide-ranging duty.

Some of the goods that were taxed included meat, salt, hats, drugs, paper, starch, glass, hops, tobacco, fish, linens and leather–a very comprehensive list.

From its very introduction the Excise aroused intense and bitter opposition. For a start it was imposed by 'ordinance', which was in effect an unconstitutional act as it had only been passed by Parliament and did not have the expressed decree of the King; it was thus considered by many to be 'revolutionary' and it suffered for many years under this ill-repute. The poor Excise officers deputed to collect the duty suffered quite considerable opposition and abuse; so much so that the Army was frequently called out to protect them. In 1647 the Excise Head Office in London was burned to the ground during a particularly savage riot against the Excise duty on meat. Despite such obvious public opposition Parliament, in 1649, described the new tax as '*the most useful and indifferent [fairly apportioned] levy that can be laid upon a people*'. Such comments suggested that the Excise was very likely to stay for many years to come.

Some of the reasons for this violent opposition were that the duty was mainly charged on the essentials of life–meat, salt, candles, leather, fish and beer–and as such it was a greater burden on the poorer members of the community, who found survival difficult enough without being taxed. Almost for the first time this section of society was forced to pay taxes–at least in an 'indirect' way. Hitherto feudal and land taxes and, indeed, Customs duties had fallen on the merchants and landed gentry. Furthermore, the tax was distrusted partly on account of its foreign origin–the Englishman's xenophobia coming to the fore. What was not forgotten for a long, long time was the original intention of the tax–to fund an army: the English had always detested the thought of a standing army.

But perhaps the most compelling reason for the hatred of the Excise was the powers of entry and search that were granted to Excise officers. At this time and throughout most of the eighteenth century, the majority of goods liable to Excise duty were made in the traders' own homes and such wide-ranging powers of entry and search breached a fundamental tenet of English life–then sanctity of one's home–a castle to be defended at all costs.

The Scottish Parliament followed their English counterparts and in 1644 introduced an Excise duty on '*everie pynt of aquavytie or strong watteris sold within the country*', which can be said to be the first duty levied on Scotch whisky. 'Biere' or beer was also made dutiable at 4d per pint. As in England, the first Excise duties were farmed–a very old system of tax collection whereby merchants and financiers leased the right to collect the duties on certain commodities in exchange for an agreed monthly or quarterly payment. This system had the advantage for the Exchequer that a certain sum was received regularly without the expense of employing collectors; the Excise farmers employed their own staff. In Scotland, however, the revenue farmers were known as 'tacksmen' and, in 1649, the Marquis of Argyll had the whole 'Tak of the Excyse' in Scotland.

There is evidence that the collection of both Customs and Excise duties in Scotland in the early days was not a great success. In 1655 Thomas Tucker, the Registrar of the English Excise, was sent to Scotland '*to give his assistance in settling the excise and customs there*'. He painted a sorry picture of most of the Scottish ports, whose trade had suffered grievously during the late wars. The Scottish Excise had made its headquarters in Leith, which was then '*the chiefe port*

MODEL OF ROBERT BURNS AS AN EXCISEMAN IN BURNS' CENTRE, DUMFRIES.

of all Scotland' and also acted as the 'nursery or gymnasium' for new recruits to the service. Smuggling was rife throughout the country, rights of exemption to the new duties abounded and Tucker found many instances of fraudulent practices amongst the many tacksmen. In the Highlands it was virtually impossible to collect the duty on spirits and ale–a situation that was to prevail for almost the next one hundred and fifty years.

Nevertheless an embryonic Scottish Excise service of sorts slowly evolved over the next few decades, although the duties never amounted to much more than £25,000–at least until the beginning of the eighteenth century. In 1683 the English Excise was taken 'out of farm' and a Board of Commissioners appointed. A national system of collection and control was established, which was managed closely by a strong London Head Office. Despite the fact that the Scottish economy had recovered from the various depredations of the Cromwellian era and was now established on a strong footing and growing prosperous, the Scottish Excise remained firmly 'in tack' until the Act of Union.

Early in 1706 Commissioners representing each country were appointed to examine the problems involved in a Union between the two countries and to agree the terms of the Treaty. The Committee resolved *'that there will be the same Customs and Excise and all other taxes and the same prohibitions, restrictions and regulations of trade throughout the United Kingdom of Great Britain.'*

When the Committee compared the revenue figures of the two countries, they found that the English Customs averaged £1¼ millions and the Excise close on to £1 million, whereas the Scottish revenues amounted to a mere £30,000 for Customs and £35,500 for the Excise. Much of the English revenue was charged to the large and quickly growing National Debt, and it was decided that it would be grossly unfair to saddle the Scottish people with a share of this burden. Therefore a system of 'equivalents' was arrived at, whereby Scotland would receive an outright cash payment of almost £400,000 and one further instalment in seven years time, the intention was to balance or redress the increased taxation which would result from the Union.

A further complication arose over the various Excise duties in force in England; some were of a temporary nature and it would be quite pointless to impose them for a short duration. However, the main duties on liquor were to be imposed straightaway and one of the other major Excise duties, that on malt, would not be imposed for another seven years. Indeed when it was finally introduced, there were serious riots, which even threatened the whole stability of the Union. Some other unpopular taxes like the duties on salt and windows were collected with very few problems.

In March 1707 the Excise Commissioners in London reported to the Treasury outlining their plans for the management of the Excise in Scotland. Not only had the Excise in Scotland been in continual tack but its collection had been anything but efficient. The system in operation was called 'composition'. This was, in effect, a rather haphazard method which was based on an estimated quantity of liquor produced in a half year on which the duty calculation was based with little or no physical check. This was quite contrary to the English system of control, with the gauging of exact quantities produced, allied to a very close survey of all the operations and premises. The Commissioners felt that to put the whole of Scotland under the same management as England would be too formidable a task, especially as so many experienced English officers would be needed to set up the new system. Rather wisely they felt that *'this may create some uneasiness'*–how right they were!

Therefore it was proposed to place Edinburgh and some of the other large trading towns under the gauging and surveying method and to continue with composition for the time being until matters were more settled and the proper Excise system extended to the whole of Scotland. Indeed, on Islay the Excise remained in tack until almost the end of the century. The London Commissioners recommended the formation of a Scottish Excise Board with a small Head Office staff exactly on the London lines. A nationwide system of collectors, supervisors and officers was proposed and because 'provisions are cheap in Scotland, the salaries of all the officials should be less than their English counterparts'.

The first Scottish Excise Board was appointed by Royal Warrant in May 1707 and took up its duties in Edinburgh in June of the same year. The five Commissioners, two less than the English Board, each received an annual salary of £300, no less than £500 below their English colleagues. The Scottish Board had far less autonomy; all their reports and duties collected had to be sent first to the English Board, who passed them on to the Treasury. Apart from William Douglas (later to be knighted), who was Brigadier-General of the Scots Dragoons, the appointees were all English Excisemen of long standing and experience. In addition, most of the important Head Office posts went to experienced London officers.

In May of the same year, twenty-six collectors and supervisors, mainly from the northern counties of England, were detached to Scotland to set up the new system. Contrary to popular belief, few of these officers stayed permanently in Scotland; by 1711 only three remained in post–as collectors. The Scottish Board had, from the outset, the power to select and appoint their own officers. All new entrants into the Service had to produce a certificate that they were *'affectionate to H.M. Queen Anne's Government'*, *'clear of the tacksman'*, of *'sober life and conversation'*, did not keep a public house and were not actively engaged in trade. This last condition prevailed for all of the eighteenth century, but still many officers managed to find a way around it as we will see later. At this early stage patronage had very little bearing on the appointments–at least as far as the Scots were concerned. Many of the officers that had served under the tacksmen were re-employed, though few survived very long as a result, no doubt, of the stricter control and discipline imposed by the new administration.

By 1710 there was a staff of thirty in Head Office, twenty-five supervisors and gaugers in Edinburgh and one hundred and ninety stationed throughout the country. In just over two years collectors had been established in Aberdeen, Ayr, Argyll, Berwick, Caithness, Dumfries, Dundee, Fife, Galloway, Glasgow, Linlithgow, Moray, Perth, Ross and Teviotdale–a very comprehensive administration. Of all the collecting staff, only twelve were known to be English. Indeed, for the next hundred years and more, virtually all the officers in the Scottish Excise bore surnames that were Scottish and mainly lowland Scottish at that. Some years ago a study was made of the Scottish Excise establishment records, which concluded that at least 95% of the collecting officers were of Scottish origins. This would seem to give the lie to the view held at the time, which has been repeated by many Scottish historians even down to this century, that Scotland was plagued by *'obnoxious English gaugers ... the influx of a horde of objectionable*

BURNS' WRITING DESK IN THE BURNS' MUSEUM, DUMFRIES.

officials ... the scum and canaglia of that country (England), who treated the natives with contempt and executed the new laws with all the vigour imaginable.' Some of the blame for this long-held but incorrect view must be shouldered by Sir Walter Scott, who wrote, *'poor auld Scotland suffers enough by thae blackguard loons o' excisemen and gaugers that has come down on her like locusts since the sad and sorrowful Union.'*

There is little doubt, however, that the attempts to impose the English system of control in the early transition period caused much trouble, and furthermore, the very presence of English officers, even though few in number, brought strong resentment and proved to be a source of bitterness for many years to come. Indeed, the term 'gauger' was used in a much more derogatory sense in Scotland than elsewhere, though in reality the Scots' main bone of contention was the existence in their midst of a new and efficient service based on the English model compared with the previous lax and rather venal system practised under the tacksmen.

One of the earliest tests for the new administration came in August 1714 with the death of Queen Anne and the advent of the German kings from Hanover. At this time particularly the threat of Jacobitism was very real and the revenue services were subjected to a most rigorous enquiry into the political affiliations of their staff. All those in Government service who were merely suspected of holding Jacobite sympathies were removed from office. The situation was bad enough in England but the changes made in the Scottish revenue services were far greater; the number of dismissals suggested a virtual witch hunt. Three out of the five Excise Commissioners found themselves out of a job, and as for the poor officers they were placed in a most difficult position. On the one hand they were very exposed to wild accusations of 'disaffection to the King' and many were discharged on very flimsy evidence–sometimes nothing more than that they had been seen 'drinking the health of the Pretender.' More often than not the information was supplied by Excise traders, who probably had private scores to settle with the officers. And yet, on the other hand, there were many instances of officers being physically abused for merely expressing their allegiance to the new King. It would appear that in some respects they could not win either way. This political tightrope that they had to walk bedeviled the Scottish Excise service right up to Burns's time and beyond. He himself had to face an enquiry into his political sympathies, caused by some anonymous and malicious informant.

The situation in Scotland worsened after the first ill-fated Jacobite Rebellion of 1715. The rebel army had, during its progress through the English northern counties, partly financed itself by collecting the Excise duties, which amounted to £380. The rebels were so well versed in the method of collection (they even issued receipts!) that it was quite obvious that some were or had been Excisemen. Certainly Ossington, the main collector of monies for the rebels, had previously been an Excise officer. This *'overt Act of Treason'*, as such action was condemned at the trials, only added fuel to the generally accepted view in London that the Scottish Excise service was riddled with Jacobite sympathisers. For the next one hundred years the Treasury maintained a strong English presence on the Scottish Board and at Head Office to ensure that there was a political stability at the head of the Service.

The new Service faced another crisis with the introduction of the malt tax. This duty had first been imposed in England in 1697 as a wartime expedient. Under the terms of the Act of Union it had first been agreed that the malt tax would not be extended to Scotland for at least seven years but this clause was later amended to 'for the duration of the war'. Most Scots were deeply concerned at the effect this new tax would have on the cost of their home-produced beer. Certainly up to the middle of the eighteenth century the most common drink was ale–quite a strong brew especially when mixed with whisky as was often the case. The Scots could not really conceive that the English would countenance a tax on their home-brewed beer in peacetime; in fact they had been re-assured that this would be the case–the malt tax was temporary! So with the War of the Spanish Succession seemingly coming to an end, the Scots had firmly convinced themselves that the malt tax would never come to Scotland.

The shock and public outcry that greeted the introduction of a bill for a Scottish malt tax, in 1713, was resounding. The Scottish lobby against the bill appeared to have failed and so strong was the opposition in Scotland that several Scottish Lords requested a personal interview with the Queen in order that they could argue the Scottish case. They pointed out that *their countrymen bore with great impatience the violation of one article of the Act of Union, that levying such an unsupportable burden as the malt tax upon them was like to raise their discontents to such a height as to prompt them to declare the Union dissolved!'* Nobody in London really put any credence on this view; it was considered overtly emotive. In any case England had the tax, so why not Scotland? The Duke of Argyll stoutly maintained, *'If this tax were to be collected in Scotland it must be done by a regiment of Dragoons!'*–an opinion which turned out to be most prescient.

The Act was passed by Parliament by a mere eight votes and the duty was introduced into Scotland at the rate of 6d per bushel, to take effect from 24th June 1713. It was estimated that there were between five and six thousand maltsters in Scotland. Even without any problems or any aggravation, it would have been a massive task for the Scottish Excise to control such a number, many of whom were situated in isolated parts of the country with very poor access. However, such was the general and determined resolution of the Scots not to submit to this new duty and to the dictate of Westminster, that the Scottish Excise had a major problem on their hands. Many officers were physically barred from entering the malthouses to survey and assess the duty. Even if they managed to gain admission to charge the duty, invariably the duty voucher was ignored and not paid; nor could the money be recovered by civil proceedings as the Justices simply refused to act in such cases. It was non-compliance on a grand scale, almost a national conspiracy, and the Excise had a hopeless task. The amount of tax collected was a mere trifle, barely sufficient to cover the cost of collection.

However bad and unsatisfactory this situation was, there was far, far worse to come. In 1725 Sir Robert Walpole decided that the existing Scottish duty should be reduced to 3d per bushel (half the rate in England) but–and this was a big but–the duty this time would be enforced by whatever force was necessary, and he confidently expected that the revenue yield would be at least £20,000.

24th June was again the fateful day and when the officers in Edinburgh attempted to collect the duty the maltsters refused them entry to their houses.

Their actions appeared to have the universal support of the people. Mobs thronged the narrow streets and lanes of the City, their cry being *'No Union, No Malt Tax.'* The Excise Head Office in the High Street of Canongate had to be barricade against the fury and violence of the mob. From Edinburgh the revolt quickly spread to the rest of Scotland. The dreaded gaugers were forced to hide for fear of their lives and at Inverness the maltsters only complied with the tax when it was harshly enforced by the military–Argyll's words had come true. The riots even spread as far as the Islands. In Orkney it was reported that the officers, whilst attempting to survey the malthouses, were soundly beaten back by *'a mob of angry and riotous women.'*

But it was in Glasgow that the most serious riots occurred. The officers were attacked and stoned and their office was ransacked, papers destroyed, and considerable damage sustained–though the rioters were prevented from burning the building down. Much of the mob's anger was directed at David Campbell, Member of Parliament for the Glasgow district of burghs. His house was plundered and the two companies of militia that were brought from Edinburgh to restore order were forced by the strongly armed mob, now five hundred strong, to retreat to Dumbarton. It took the intervention of General Wade himself, marching at the head of his regiment, to bring order to Glasgow. Several of the rioters were transported and many more were publicly whipped. Some members of the City Corporation were heavily fined, as it was felt that they had not done enough to prevent the riots and the City was compelled to recompense the Excise Commissioners for the damage sustained to their property. With some minor relaxations the malt tax was eventually enforced–but never with any ease. It was agreed that part of the revenue collected would be applied to a scheme to improve Scottish trade and commerce. Nevertheless, the severity with which the 'Glasgow Malt Insurrection' (as it became known) was put down by the military rankled with the Scots for many a long day and gave them just another reason to hate 'The English Excise and their damned gaugers' and all they stood for.

Twenty years later there was another serious disturbance to the Scottish Excise when the second Jacobite Rebellion erupted in 1745. Following the pattern of the earlier uprising, the rebels again collected the Excise duties as they advanced through England. By the time the force had reached Derby they had appropriated well over £2,000. In this instance there was positive proof that officers from both the Customs and Excise services had joined the rebel army. Most of the officers had enlisted in Edinburgh. Many had been seen 'drinking treasonable healths' and heard 'speaking disrespectfully of HRH the Duke of Cumberland'. There was no shortage of people prepared to come forward to give evidence against the gaugers and as had been the case thirty years earlier, many officers were dismissed. Henceforth all officers had to be very circumspect in the views they expressed especially when they were 'in their cups'!

In May 1746, after the defeat at Culloden, the Excise supervisors were given the invidious task of compiling lists of persons in their districts who were known to have helped or sided with the rebels. The returns, which have survived, gave full names and addresses, occupations, and details of the whereabouts of the persons named (though the majority are shown rather cryptically as *'lurking')*) and the evidence to support this information. In very many cases it was the gaugers who supplied the vital information and in quite a few instances they were also responsible for capturing the rebels. The lists name no fewer than 2,520 persons, mainly from the Highlands. Very few of this number are shown as 'believed killed.' The lists emphasise that it was no light matter to wear a white cockade, drink toasts without due reflection, or speak disrespectfully of King George. Perhaps it is not really very surprising that the Highlanders especially considered the Excise gaugers as interfering officials who should be hindered and hampered at every turn and that no opportunity should be lost to evade the various duties they collected.

In whatever part of Scotland the Excise officers found themselves stationed they were faced with smuggling on a really massive scale. Strangely it was only in Scotland that the word 'smuggling' was used to cover not only the illegal importation of goods but also the illicit distillation of spirits. Smuggling (in both senses) in Scotland had been for many, many years a national pastime–a good and honest trade harming nobody but the Government. The rapid and penal rises in Customs duties since the Union, however, and the gradual but steady increase in the Excise duty on spirits allied to the detested malt tax, only added as a spur to the smuggling trade. The Scottish smuggling trade had an added dimension in that it was considered a direct blow to the Act of Union.

From the Solway right around to the Berwick coast the free trade in tea, tobacco, brandy, geneva, wines and salt flourished. The south-west coast was the centre of large-scale smuggling. It was here that it became very highly organised with large and well-armed vessels of up to 300 tons regularly landing sizeable quantities of goods on commission for several established 'smuggling merchants,' who controlled the area. The goods came from the Isle of Man, which was a veritable smuggling haven, Ireland, the Channel Isles and often from France. In 1765, however, the Duke of Atholl, sold his feudal rights as Lord of Man to the Crown. The Revestment Act effectively curbed the independence of the Isle of Man and severely restricted its smuggling activities, though they were by no means eradicated. It was in the south-west that Customs cutters made their first appearance in Scottish waters, though quite soon other vessels would be stationed at the east coasts ports from Inverness to Dunbar. The smuggling vessels operating on this coast took their cargoes at Flushing, Ostend or Copenhagen. The Excise Commissioners described the situation: *'(they) are armed in the strongest manner with carriage guns and swivel guns and small arms … they come openly, in the daytime, often in pairs with a determined and strong resolution of running their cargoes under force of arms, or of resisting, to blood and death, every attempt by our officers to prevent them.'*

It was not until 1763 that the Scottish Excise had their own vessels. These were the largest and most strongly armed revenue vessels afloat and, as such, were particularly successful. They captured on average five smuggling vessels a year. The Excise cruisers were used to good effect against the illicit distillers. They would cruise close in to the coast and at the first sign of tell-tale smoke, a boat would be lowered and the crew would race to the scene only to find, in most instances, that the smugglers had disappeared leaving their still, which of course would be destroyed by the Excise. Virtually all the vessels that served under the two Scottish Boards were named after Royal personages. Perhaps the Scottish

RIVER NITH AT DUMFRIES.

Commissioners were more royalist than their English counterparts, who favoured such names as *Greyhound, Vigilant, Active, Swift* etc. Probably the Commissioners felt that because of the political situation in Scotland for most of the century, their vessels should openly proclaim their Royal authority.

For many generations illicit distillation had been part and parcel of Scottish life. The Highlanders, especially, had used their barley, their water and their peat to produce their own individual spirit and they saw no good reason why any Government gauger should interfere and change the habits of a lifetime. Indeed, on many small Highland crofts the sale of 'highland dew' struck the fine balance between survival and starvation, and often the profits of the illicit still paid for the rents.

The extent of illicit distillation during the eighteenth century is quite impossible to assess and will never be known. It has often been stated that around Glenlivet alone there were no fewer than 200 illicit stills, and certainly smuggling was not confined to the Highlands. The Lowland distiller was close to hand for the ready markets of the larger towns without the profitable trade across the border into England. In 1777 it was reckoned that in Edinburgh there were at least 400 illicit stills. During the course of the 1780's over 6,000 illicit stills were seized and destroyed by the Excise and no doubt this was just the tip of the iceberg. Most legal distilleries in the nineteenth century were very proud to claim their origin as 'on the site of an illicit still'!

Evidence given to the Committee on Scottish Distilleries in 1798 suggested a wholesale disregard of the Excise laws: *'the distillery in Scotland is in a thousand hands ... not confined to great towns but it spreads itself over the whole face of the country and in every island from Orkney to Jura ... a great deal of spirits are distilled both for sale and for private use. The injury the revenue sustains is very considerable.'* Indeed the Excise never really got to grips with the problem until after 1823 when there were widespread changes in the legislation and a very close Excise system of control was imposed.

There was a rather strange anomaly in operation for most of the century. Duncan Forbes of Culloden had lands at Ferintosh, where his 'ancient brewry of Aqua Vitae' was laid to waste in 1688. As compensation Forbes was allowed to distil spirits at Ferintosh for one annual payment, which by 1780 only amounted to some £72 per year. Yet by this time his distillery was producing in excess of 100,000 gallons a year on which the Excise duty would have been in the region of £20,000. Ferintosh was a good whisky and sold throughout Scotland and England, indeed in London there was a special warehouse established to cope with the trade. The Excise Commissioners quite rightly complained to the Treasury that *'Mr. Forbes distilled in a manner as if duty free'* and they tried on several occasions to get the concession withdrawn. Finally, in 1784, Forbes's exemption from Excise duty on spirits was brought to an end with a lump sum payment of £21,000 from the Treasury–not bad compensation. Robert Burns was moved to write–

> Thee Ferintosh! O sadly lost!
> Scotland lament from coast to coast!
> Now colic grips, an barkin hoast
> > May kill us a';
> For loyal Forbes' charter'd toast
> > Is ta'en awa!

Scotch Drink (C.W.p.167)

An extra burden to all these smuggling problems was the violence shown to those officers who attempted to seize either the illicit stills or the smuggled goods. Sometimes, if they were fortunate, the officers had the help of dragoons, but more often than not they were on their own or in small parties of three or four, sadly outnumbered when faced with large gangs of determined, desperate and well-armed smugglers, who would be prepared to stop at nothing in order that they and their goods would not be taken. As the penalties for smuggling became more and more draconian, the opposition became more fierce and the incidence of violence more commonplace. It is perhaps understandable that many officers, if not actually in collusion with the smugglers (though some undoubtedly were), connived at their activities in their area.

Thus the lot of Scottish Excise officers in the eighteenth century was not a particularly happy one. They and their families lived and worked in an alien and largely hostile community, where often the wives and children were harassed and intimidated by the local people. In some areas the officers were often in personal danger. Excise work was long and physically arduous especially considering the Scottish climate. They suffered frequent removes of area (often every four years) with all the attendant problems of finding suitable accommodation. By and large they were universally distrusted and in many areas they were actively hated. They were expected to collect very unpopular taxes in an efficient manner and to enforce the many and various complicated Excise laws with equality and equanimity. Furthermore they were closely monitored and strictly managed by their superiors and were expected to work to a very high standard. They were restricted as to the friends they could make in the community and had to take great care over what they said or wrote. All this for a mere £50 per annum! And yet there was never a shortage of recruits into the Service ... one wonders why?

Chapter Two

In 1787, the year that Burns's thoughts were turning on the strong possibility of an Excise career, the Scottish Excise service had been in existence for eighty years. It is appropriate to review its progress since the Union because that fatal step still figured largely in its affairs. Somewhat quaintly all the Scottish Excise records and accounts were notated as '...th year'–so many years after Michaelmas 1707; in this way the Service and its officers were constantly, indeed almost daily, reminded of the Union.

Thus, in its 80th year the Service had survived the painful traumas of its early years and the vicissitudes of the Jacobite period to develop into a soundly based, well organised and strongly managed administration. This position had been achieved in spite of all the problems of collection–large scale non-compliance, poor roads, inferior communications and, of course, smuggling. The collecting staff now numbered some five hundred and twenty officers of various grades, well over double the initial complement. These officers were responsible for a bewildering array of duties–auctions, beer, bricks, candles, cocoa, coffee, cider, glass, hides and skins, malt, paper, printed calico, soap, spirits, tea, tobacco, wine and wire. The average annual total of revenue collected came to over £400,000. Needless to say the head office establishment in Edinburgh had also grown with a proliferation of clerks to control and manage the seemingly endless mass of returns, reports, vouchers and accounts demanded by the Board from their officers.

It is no idle boast to claim that both the English and Scottish Excise were considered the most efficient of all the revenue services. They had recently undergone rigorous and searching enquiries by several Parliamentary committees and not only had they escaped relatively unscathed but they had even received praise and credit for their able administration and the low costs of collection of the many and varied duties under their charge. Unlike the Customs service there were no patent or sinecure posts. Indeed, the employment of deputies in the Excise was strictly forbidden. The Customs also had an elaborate and most lucrative system of fees, which lent itself to abuse and corruption; whereas there were very few allowable fees in the Excise. But perhaps the most important difference between the two services was that the Excise had a well-established avenue of promotion based solely on merit, which led to the top post of collector. All levels of the Service in the collections were filled by experienced officers, thus making the Excise a highly professional service. On the other hand

THE OLD EXCISE HEAD OFFICE IN EDINBURGH.

the chief Customs posts of collector and controller were not open to promotion for serving officers but were always filled by inexperienced persons from outside the service and could only be obtained through patronage.

The organisation of the Excise in Scotland was relatively simple and followed the English pattern. The whole of the country was divided into a number of areas called 'collections', and at this particular time they numbered twenty, one of which had its headquarters at Dumfries. The officer placed in charge of this area was designated the collector. Throughout Burns's time in the Excise he was based in the Dumfries collection and his collector was John Mitchell. (Check numbered twenty above)

Each collection was further divided into smaller areas known as 'districts', which were controlled by 'supervisors'. In Dumfries collection there were two such districts–Wigtown and Dumfries itself. Burns served under two supervisors–John Rankine until his death in 1791 and then Alexander Findlater, who became his firm friend and the staunch defender of his reputation after his death. Burns considered Findlater to be *'one of the worthiest fellows in the universe'*(C.L.p.439).

There was a major difference in the functions of the collector and supervisor. The latter was in the immediate management of the officers. He checked their work and accounts and advised them on the legal and technical aspects of the various Excise duties. However, he had no responsibility for the physical collection of the revenue. The collector was obviously the superior officer and apart from being responsible for all the officers and supervisors his primary function, as his title suggests, was physically to collect the Excise duties from the various traders, assessed by the officers. Ultimately, of course, the collector was directly accountable to the Commissioners in Edinburgh for the proper management of his staff and his collection.

The districts themselves were further sub-divided into 'stations' and these were the basic units of Excise administration. This is where the myriad of Excise laws and regulations were enforced and the duties assessed. Each station was in charge of an officer or 'gauger' (as Burns preferred to call himself). The officer was solely responsible for the control and correct assessment of all the Excise duties arising within his area. If the stations were either sited in a town or sufficiently close to a town to provide enough official work within a small radius the stations were known as 'foot-walks.' But if a town was large enough to have more than one station they were then called 'divisions' and during Burn's time Dumfries comprised three divisions. Rural Excise stations that covered wide areas and thus involved a considerable amount of riding were called 'itineraries' and contained a certain number of 'rides'. It was normal for an officer to be first appointed to a ride station and then progress to a town foot-walk before he could even be considered for promotion. The theory behind this was that there was a far greater number of Excise traders in towns and also they were more likely to offer a greater variety and complexity of work than those in the country areas. So the ride stations could almost be considered training stations for the new officers.

Excise officers were also employed in the ports as either 'port officers' or 'port gaugers'. Here they assessed and calculated the Excise duties on imported goods and checked and controlled the export of goods where drawback (refund) of duty was being claimed. During the previous decade there had been many

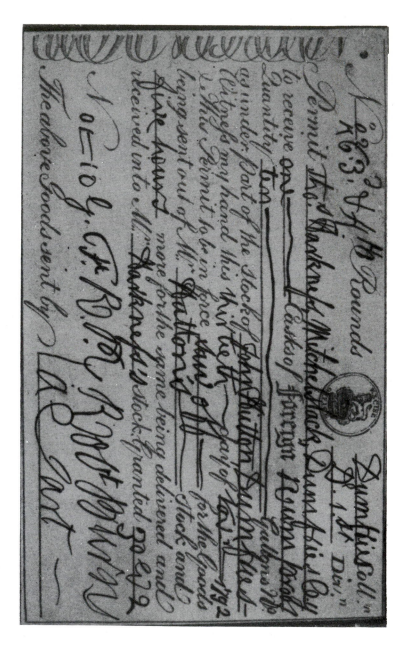

EXCISE PERMIT FOR RUM SIGNED BY BURNS. (HMSO).

changes in the methods of charging and collecting duty on imported goods. A system of Excise bonded (i.e duty-free) warehouses had been introduced and many goods previously liable to high Customs duties were now liable to a mixture of Excise and Customs duties–tea, tobacco and spirits were the prime examples. It was considered that as the Excise was a more efficient and less corrupt service the amount of revenue collected by this radical change should greatly improve with less incidence of fraud. Dumfries was, of course, a port albeit a relatively minor one, but it did have one port officer who was responsible in the main for tobacco imports. Burns spent nearly two years in this post.

The basic system of Excise control in a station was that any person who proposed to carry on any excisable trade–brewer, maltster, tanner, paper maker, brick maker, chandler, distiller etc–was required by law to declare to the officer the premises at which he intended to work and also to list the various vessels and utensils which he proposed to use in his trade. The trader, if his proposals were satisfactory to the Excise, was granted a licence to carry on his trade and was thus brought into the Excise 'net' and henceforth under the control and survey of the officer. Some Excise traders complained that they could not cough without first notifying the officer!

From then on the trader was strictly regulated and he was compelled to notify the officer in writing before he commenced any manufacturing operation. Furthermore he was required to declare the quantity of materials to be used in an operation. For instance, in the case of a maltster, the precise quantity of barley to be laid on the floor of the malthouse, or the chandler, the total amount of tallow placed in the vats for making candles and so on. The officer was then required, largely at his own discretion as to timing, to visit the premises and examine the 'entry' made in the trader's books and generally satisfy himself as to the correctness of the declaration. Also he was expected to visit the premises frequently during the manufacturing process at different times, both during the day and night, to ensure that no undeclared activity or fraud was taking place. At the end of each visit or 'survey' he was compelled to leave full details of the conditions of the vessels and the work that he had done. With some Excise trades the officer also had to attend to unlock the vats and vessels as they were kept under Excise lock and seal not in use. One Excise officer said that he '*gave the appearance of a turnkey of a prison, so numerous were the keys I carried.*'

The system of the actual collection of Excise duties had not changed since the introduction of the duty and would not alter in essence until the middle of the next century. The Excise collectors went on 'the rounds' of their collections eight times a year, and held 'sitting days' at each of the market towns in their areas. Unlike the Customs where every port had a Custom House for the receipt of duties, there were few Excise offices as such and most officers worked from home. Therefore the collector usually held his 'sitting days' at inns, the publicans were designated 'office-keepers' and held a deputation from the Excise Board to receive entries and notices submitted by Excise traders. The appointment of an inn as an Excise office was highly sought after for not only did this lend approbation to the house, it also guaranteed a brisk trade during the sitting days! All the Excise traders were required to attend these sittings to pay the duty that had accrued in the previous weeks. The actual amount of duty due had been calculated by the officers from their surveys and notified to the trader and collector by the issue of a duty voucher.

One of the many problems faced by Excise collectors was the safeguarding of the monies they had collected on their rounds. Although they were normally armed with pistols and were attended by either a clerk or a young supernumary officer, there are frequent instances of collectors being attacked and one was even murdered. Collectors were expressly forbidden by the Board 'to ride between dusk and dawn', which created problems in Scotland during the winter months.

The Excise officer's responsibilities did not end with the control of licensed Excise traders. He had to ensure that there were no illicit operations in his area. During the eighteenth century most Scottish farmers malted their own barley and the majority attempted to avoid paying the much detested duty. Also many innkeepers brewed their own beer without licence and although home-produced beer was not liable to duty, beer sold at fairs was and the brewing of 'bye-beer' (as it was called) caused problems in Scotland. And, of course, over and above this was the constant search for illicit stills. But perhaps the most onerous and time-consuming aspect of an officer's life was checking the dealers in various excisable goods. By law all spirit and wine merchants, tobacconists and tea dealers were required to be licensed. They had to keep an accurate stock record and were not allowed to remove goods (even if they were duty-paid) without a permit issued by the officers. As part of their control of the dealers the officers were required physically to check the dealer's stocks regularly and monitor his records and accounts. This close control was an attempt to prevent smuggled goods being sold through normal trade channels; if goods were being moved on the road without a permit it was assumed that they were smuggled and therefore liable to seizure.

As if all this practical work was not sufficient, at the end of the day the officer had to maintain a journal of all his visits or surveys, up-date his ledgers of the traders, write out reports and complete duty returns and vouchers. He also needed to keep abreast of the various changes in Excise legislation. It was not until the year after Burns's death that the first complete abstract of Excise laws was published; this 'abridgement' comprised a mere nine hundred pages! So complicated had the legislation become that an Excise Commissioner averred that *'no one man can have mastery over the laws of the Excise.'* Nevertheless should an officer slip up as a result of ignorance of the appropriate law he was quickly brought to book and usually reprimanded. Officers like Burns had to obtain their knowledge and guidance on the law by painstakingly plodding through Acts of Parliament, copies of general letters from the Board, fragmentary memoranda and notes made from verbal instructions. To find a path through eighteenth century Excise legislation was no mean achievement.

An Excise Commissioner in the early days of the Scottish service wisely remarked, *'due knowledge and choice of officers is one of the essential parts of the duty of this Commission'.* Fine words but just how did they go about selecting them? Perhaps it would be more accurate to ask how they allocated persons to posts as there is no evidence of a system of selection–certainly not as one would accept the meaning today.

During the eighteenth century there was an unwritten law as far as England

8r 2	Alexr Dickson	Do	5 Jan 1793	27 Nov 1793 Lanark	John Reid Aberdeen 8
8r 2	Chas Gorden	Do	6 Aprl 1793	27 Jan 1794 Leith 2d	Robt McCracken Jnl
8r 2	Gray Campbell	Do	15 May Do	2 Jan 1794 Caithness	Thomas Ross Fe
8r 2	Adam Whyte	Do	3 June Do	13 June 1793 Argyl M	Thomas Spens Nov
8r 2	Henry Hannah	Do	3 June Do	Leith Brewery	Alex Stenhouse Feb
June 8	Jas McFarlane	Do	3 June Do	4 Feby 1795 Haddington	
Augt 11	Jas Tweedie	Do	3 June Do	Edinr Brewery	
Sep 30	Robt Carrick	Mr Dundas	17 June Do	1 Oct 1794 Oldmeldrum	
Nov 13	Angus McDonald	Board	19 June Do	24 Nov 1794 Lanark	
8r 18	Jas Hunter	Treasury	26 Nov 1792	Struck off	
Jan 2 1793	John Scott	Do	4 Feb 1793	Struck off	
Aprl 17	Jas White	Do	16 Dec 1793	14 Jan 1795 Deorder	
Sep 21	John Fotheringham	Do	23 Jan 1794	3 Sept 1796 Lithgow	
8r 29	Hugh Hunter	Board	10 Feb 1794	7 July 1796 Dumblane	
Nov 25	Gavin Frazer	Do	11 Oct 1794	26 Aug 1796 Alloa	
Dec 12	Robt Barclay	Do	22 Dec 1794	24 Sept 1796 Dado	
Jan 16 1790	Wm Comrie	Treasury	16 Feb 1795	7 Dec 1796 Canon Brewy	
June 14	Jas Fletcher	Board	14 Aprl 1795	5 Jan 1797 Wigton	
July 25	Jas Mitchell	Do	3 Sept 1795	12 Jan 1797 Alloa	
Nov 19	Thos Stewart	Do	1 Aug 1796	13 Apr 1797 Kinky	
Dec 15	Alexr Gilles	Do	26 Sept 1796	6 May 1797 Kilmarnock	
Jan 27 1791	John Maitland	Do	12 Oct 1796	June 1797 Hamilton	
8r 27	Robt Burns	Do	Secd		
Feb 1	Jas Lindsay	Do	12 Jan 1797	10 Augt 1797 Dumblane	
Do 1	Duncn Forbes	Do	20 Apr 1797	7 Aug 1797 Wigton	
	Robt Neilson	Do	22 Dec 1796	1797 Wigton	

EXCISE REGISTER OF OFFICERS PUT ON THE LIST FOR EXAMINER
AND SUPERVISOR. (HMSO).

was concerned that one third of the posts in the various revenue services were 'in the hands' of the Treasury, one third with the Commissioners and the reminder filled from recommendations made by serving staff. In the Customs only collectors and controllers, to a lesser degree, had any influence. In Scotland, however, there is some evidence to suggest that the Treasury were not so involved in the appointments with the result that the Scottish Commissioners had more influence over the appointment of staff. It was a fact of life that the amount of patronage the Commissioners held made a seat on one of the revenue boards one of the most coveted prizes of eighteenth century political life.

In the Excise, both in England and Scotland, there appeared to be almost a deliberate policy to favour the relatives of serving officers. Indeed at one period when there was a long waiting list for Excise posts the Commissioners instructed that in future, *'only the relatives of serving officers would be considered.'* This merely re-enforced the already very strong family links of service in the Excise, which prevailed up to fairly modern times. Certainly in the Scottish Excise it is not unusual to find up to five generations serving in the Excise.

If we merely consider some of Burns's colleagues this strong family tradition is clearly shown. John Mitchell, his collector, although the son of a tenant farmer, had an uncle who was a supervisor and he, himself, married the sister of a supervisor. James Findlay, who instructed Burns, was the son of an Exciseman as was Alexander Findlater, his supervisor. Also for good measure one of Findlater's brothers followed him into the Excise, as did two of Findlater's sons. John Lewars, close friend of Burns in his Dumfries days, was the son of a supervisor and John's son entered the Excise. Finally Adam Stobie, the young man who undertook Burns's work during his last fatal illness, was the son of an officer as was his younger brother James. It should not be assumed, however, that a family connection automatically ensured an Excise appointment because there are several instances of such applications being refused. For example John McQuaker, another colleague of Burns at Dumfries, applied unsuccessfully in 1801 for his son John to be admitted to the Service. Perhaps the reason for the refusal was that the father was not considered a particularly diligent officer–he was considered to be only 'a middling officer'.

It would be grossly unfair to suggest that the Scottish Excise suffered under nepotism. The system of recruitment from existing staff had proved to work very well. It had several advantages for the Excise Board. The Commissioners were well aware of the family background of the entrant, who would have been inculcated into the standards of behaviour and performance demanded by the Board. Also, of course, they would be well trained in all the intricacies of the work by their fathers. The system maintained the strong *esprit de corps*, which was such a feature of both the English and Scottish Excise–colleagues became firm friends, they addressed one another as 'brother' and there are many instances of them bequeathing gifts and property to colleagues. Possibly because of their isolation in the community they exhibited a proud and sometimes belligerent determination to stand by one another. Young Adam Stobie's fine gesture of refusal of salary during Burns's illness is a good example as was Jessie Lewar's attention during Burns's last days.

If one was not fortunate enough to have any Excise relatives, however, the next best thing was to come from a family directly involved in an Excise trade.

Many officers were the sons of brewers, merchants, vintners and, yes, even maltsters. Such entrants had, at least, some basic knowledge and experience of Excise procedure as it affected the family business and perhaps they were even recommended by the local officer or supervisor. John Gillespie, the unsuccessful suitor of Burns's Chloris came from a family of shipping merchants and Adam Pearson, the man who signed Burns's Excise commission came from a well-known brewing family, although perhaps the fact that his mother was related to James Balmain, the Excise Commissioner, may explain why he was appointed Secretary–one of the top posts in the Excise administration. William Younger, the founder of the brewing dynasty, was a very successful Exciseman from 1753 until his death in harness in 1770. His brewery in Leith, which he founded in 1747, was actually managed by his wife Grizel because his official post obviously precluded him from taking an active role.

The very first step for any prospective Excise candidate, whoever he might be, was to obtain a certificate, which was duly signed and authenticated by a serving Excise official at collector or supervisor level. In Burns's first letter to Robert Graham, the Excise Commissioner, which he wrote in January 1788 the certificate is mentioned, 'I have, according to form, been examined by a Supervisor and I give in his Certificate with a request for an Order for instruction ...' (C.L.p.424). Like so many other Excise records relating to Burns this certificate unfortunately has not survived. It has been suggested that it was completed by the supervisor at Ayr–the nearest district to Mauchline–prior to Burns's visit to Edinburgh. I think it more likely, however, to have been signed by William Nimmo, Supervisor at Lanark district. Burns was known to be a regular visitor to Nimmo's house in Alison Square, Edinburgh. It is my feeling that Nimmo could have had a considerable influence on Burns's decision to apply for an Excise post. Nimmo had served for a long time in the Scottish Excise and must have been well-known at the Head Office. Indeed the executor of his will was none other than Adam Pearson, the Excise Secretary. Of course it was on 4th December 1787 that Burns attended a tea party at Alison Square hosted by Nimmo's sister, Erskine, the fatal first meeting with Mrs. Agnes McLehose–Clarinda.

The form of certificate had been in use in the Excise since the start of the century and had remained virtually unchanged since its introduction. It certified that the applicant was above twenty-one and under thirty years of age (proof of this had to be produced) and whether the candidate was single or not, and if married had a family no larger than a wife and two children. Furthermore, he was asked whether he understood the first four rules of 'vulgar and decimal arithmetick' and was of the Communion of the Church of Scotland. Information was needed as to his previous occupation and 'what business he followed.' The applicant had to provide the names of two securities to answer to £200 'for the due execution of his office.' Finally, the certificate had to be completed in the applicant's handwriting. The examinee, as he was called, noted the name of the officer by whom the applicant wished to be instructed and confirmed that he, himself, had not accepted any fee or inducement to obtain the appointment.

The completed certificate, accompanied by a nomination from the sponsor was forwarded to the Excise Board, who would consider the application and listen to any evidence against the applicant. If the Commissioners approved the candidate they would issue an order, through their Secretary, for the entrant to be properly instructed by the nominated officer. A supervisor was required to examine the candidate closely after his instruction and to his satisfaction. Then, and only then, would the entrant be accepted into the Service as an 'expectant;' in other words he would be placed on a list to await the next ride vacancy. As we will see later Burns was able, through the good offices of his patron, Robert Graham, to short-circuit the system and be appointed directly to an Excise station without becoming an expectant. More to the point, he was appointed to a station where he was actually living at the time, which was a very rare occurrence. Thus, to any candidate the active interest of a Commissioner was all important and to retain his support and protection throughout one's career was equally vital as Burns was later to discover.

Patronage was a recognisable and widely accepted part of eighteenth century society; it abounded and permeated all walks of life. But it was in the revenue services that its use and abuse were more readily seen. Unfortunately it remained a potent force in the Civil Service until the reforms of Northcote and Trevelyan in the mid-nineteenth century. Dr. Johnson's view of a patron as 'commonly a wretch who supports with insolence and is paid with flattery' is perhaps a somewhat cynical opinion but this was at a time when patronage was at its height. By the 1820's a slightly different view was being taken. When Canning pointed out to Sir Walter Scott, after he had commended his son-in-law John Lockhart (a biographer of Burns) for an Excise post, that it was one thing to do a favour for oneself but quite another matter to ask a third party to do it for you, Canning was merely expressing a new type of morality that was surfacing in public life. William Cobbett, in 1829, was far more forthright with his advice to young men, '... to look not for success to favour, to partiality, to friendship or what is called interest ...' Sadly Burns had no such free choice in the matter. The path he had elected to follow demanded the interest of an influential person and although he has been roundly condemned by some critics for the sycophantic tone of his letters to his patrons, Burns was merely following the rules of the game. Burns not only accepted the system, despite all its faults, but manipulated it to his very best advantage.

Burns's main patron and constant supporter as far as the Excise was concerned was Robert Graham, the 12th Laird of Fintry. The Graham family could trace their ancestry back to Robert III; indeed, the family was steeped in Scottish history. However, they had fallen on relatively hard times and although Graham was forced to sell his estate he still retained his title. Perhaps because of his impecunious situation Graham obtained an appointment as Excise Commissioner in Edinburgh in January 1787. Burns first met his future patron at Blair Atholl on 31st August 1787 when the poet was being entertained by the fourth Duke of Athole while on his Highland tour. It would appear that Burns was immediately impressed with, 'Mr. Graham of Fintrie's charms of conversation' (C.L.p.354). During the two days that Burns was at Athole House he would have found much to discuss with Graham. The Excise Commissioner was a well-read man and had attended the University of St. Andrews at the same time as Robert Fergusson, the famous poet. Burns would have been eager to hear at first hand of the man he considered his master and who had the greatest influence on his poetry. Furthermore, Graham had a reputation as a ladies' man—there had been a hint of a scandal with him and the Countess of Strathmore—so there was likely to be an affinity of feeling between the two men. Just twelve months later Burns was effusive in his praise of Graham, 'one of the worthiest and most accomplished gentleman not only of this country but, I will dare to say it, of this age.'

Robert Graham remained the poet's steady friend and patron for the rest of Burns's life, as the three poetic epistles and the numerous letters fully testify. Graham was able to bestow his patronage without offending such an independent and proud individual as Burns–no mean feat! In a letter to 'the beautiful' Mrs. Graham in June 1790 Burns summed up his thoughts on patronage;

> It is not my fault that I was born to dependence; nor is it Mr.
> Graham's chiefest praise that he can command influence; but it is his
> merit to bestow with the politeness of a gentleman and the kindness
> of a Brother, and I trust it is mine to receive with ingenuous
> thankfulness and to remember with undiminished gratitude.
>
> (C.L.p.555)

Burns was also particularly fortunate in his other patron–James Cunningham, the 14th Earl of Glencairn. The Earl's factor, Alexander Dalziel, was responsible for introducing the Earl to the works of Burns. Consequently when Burns arrived in Edinburgh in 1786 with a letter of introduction, the Earl was able to open many doors for him. The Earl became his Edinburgh patron and introduced him into the top social and literary circles in the City. In January 1788 Burns wrote to Glencairn asking for his assistance in obtaining an Excise post. However, it is not known what effect, if any, the Earl's solicitation had on the Excise Board; I suspect that it was nothing more than a welcome support to Graham's nomination. The great admiration and respect Burns felt for 'his Titular Protector' was very genuine and deep, as his elegy on the Earl's untimely death conveys–

But I'll remember thee, Glencairn
And a'that thou has done for me!

Lament For James, Earl Of Glençairn (C.W.p.425)

Burns almost, but not quite, had another powerful patron–Adam Smith, the famous economist and Scottish Customs Commissioner. Smith came from a family that had a long Customs background. His grandfather and father had both been Controllers in Kirkcaldy and his uncle had been the Collector at the same port for a number of years. In 1778, just two years after *The Wealth of Nations* was first published, Adam Smith was appointed to a seat on the Scottish Customs Board and he remained a Commissioner until his death in 1790.

Although Adam Smith had subscribed for four copies of the Edinburgh edition of Burns's poems and was probably the most notable figure in Edinburgh, the two famous literary men were never destined to meet. For most of the winter of 1786/7 (Burns's first visit to the City) Adam Smith was seriously ill and confined to his house so he did not attend any of the literary and social gatherings where the young poet was lionised. It would appear that Adam Smith considered offering Burns a Customs post as a salt officer. The salary of this position varied between £30 and £40 with the possibility of fees to double that amount. The duties were relatively light, which would have allowed Burns time to devote to his literary work. Smith also considered that such a position held less odium than the Excise.

Mrs. Dunlop, an acquaintance of Adam Smith, wrote to Burns in Edinburgh on 26th February 1787 informing him of the Commissioner's thoughts and enclosing

LETTER TO ROBERT GRAHAM OF FINTRY 25th MARCH 1788 re: EXCISE INSTRUCTION.
(NATIONAL LIBRARY OF SCOTLAND)

a letter of introduction to the famous man. When Burns replied on 22nd March he said that when he called at Smith's house (Panmure House in Canongate), 'Dr. Smith was just gone to London the morning before I rec'd your letter to him' (C.L.p.136). It is certainly known that Adam Smith was in London on 21st March as he went there to consult his doctor–the famous John Hunter. Thus they never met, missing each other by a mere twenty-four hours. How different Burns's life might have turned out if he had entered the Customs service instead of the Excise.

It would therefore almost seem that Burns was pre-destined to become an Exciseman. By the purest chance he had met Robert Graham, while the Commissioner just happened to be a fellow guest at Blair Atholl–a very long coincidence. Graham was the only Excise Commissioner that Burns had any contact with, at least prior to his acceptance into the service. The other members of the Board–George Brown, Thomas Wharton, James Stodart, and James Balmain–are not mentioned in any of Burns's letters nor were they likely to be encountered in the society that feted Burns during his first winter in Edinburgh. The many influential new friends he made during this time were unlikely to help him gain an Excise post. In their view literary genius should not be sullied by taking up gauging tools and the 'Heaven-taught ploughman-poet' (a *persona* Burns carefully fostered) should remain at the plough. It should also be noted that Burns just scraped in on the strict age rule; in fact he was over thirty years of age when he took up the appointment. There is no doubt that any other candidate with the same family background as Burns would not have gained an appointment.

Burns had a most compelling reason to enter the Excise–it would provide him with a regular income to support himself and his growing family. However, some explanation is needed to understand why so many young men were virtually queuing up to gain the coveted appointment in a Service despite all the apparent drawbacks. *The Royal Gauger,* the standard work on Excise procedure in the eighteenth century, warned aspiring officers that, 'notwithstanding there are several vacancies every week, yet there are so many applying that those petitioners who have the best Solicitors always soonest succeed.' And yet this throng of hopeful Excisemen seemed undaunted by the long hours, the physically arduous work, its attendant dangers and, indeed, the unpopularity of the Service.

The main attraction was, of course, the salary. A ride officer commanded £50 per annum and this sum compared very favourably with other callings. For instance, the majority of curates were on stipends which varied between £30 and £45. Tutors were very fortunate to earn a similar figure and even the assistants to professors at the universities were only paid £60 per year. Certainly the majority of clerks in towns other than Edinburgh and Glasgow had to eke out a living on far less than an officer received; their average income was £45 per annum, quite close to that of cotton spinners, who were then amongst the highest paid skilled workers in Scotland.

Thomas Paine, the author of *The Rights of Man* and *The Age of Reason* and an Excise officer from 1762 to 1774, had published a pamphlet in 1772 on the inadequacy of officers' pay. He had cogently argued the case for some increase in salary. Paine maintained that after deductions for tax, the charity fund and expenses of a horse, the salary amounted to a mere £32 or one shilling and ninepence farthing per day! His appeal fell on deaf ears; the English Excise Board felt that as they could obtain any number of men to fill the posts there was no call to raise the salary. Paine was not particularly surprised at this reaction; as he commented, 'A rebellion of Excisemen, who seldom have the populace on their side, is unlikely to succeed.' On the other hand Burns found the salary much more congenial, 'I find £50 per annum, an exceeding good thing' (C.L.p.498). However, compared with the unprofitable business of farming at Ellisland, this comment is not too surprising. In any case the cost of living in Scotland was quite appreciably lower than in England.

Another benefit of the salary was that it was regular and paid each month and unlike most jobs it was not governed by fluctuations in business or trade; or in Burns's case not dictated by the vagaries of the weather on the outcome of the harvest. Furthermore the security of the tenure of an Excise post was not an inconsiderable advantage. Providing an officer acted sensibly, worked reasonably diligently, avoided excessive drinking and steered clear of politics, he had a job for life. Although many officers were discharged for a variety of misdemeanours, all of their own making, none had been made redundant because of a fall-off in work.

The basic salary was not the whole story though, as there were ample opportunities to augment one's income. The obvious method was by rewards for seizing smuggled goods. Officers were entitled to one half of the proceeds of the sale of smuggled goods and until the early decades of the nineteenth century an officer could receive £25 for every convicted smuggler. And in the case of more mundane 'technical' Excise offences, officers were allowed one half of the Court fines. This was a much easier method of earning extra money due to the very complex Excise legislation. However, the officer had to pay the Court costs out of his sum and this usually meant dining the Justices! There is no doubt that an active and zealous officer could easily increase his salary by no small amount. Indeed William Younger, who was a first-rate seizing officer, regularly doubled his annual salary. In one year alone he received two separate sums of £55 and £79 as a result of large tobacco seizures. It is perhaps a rather wry thought to consider that Excise money helped to support his first brewery! As we will see later Burns's income was likely to be more than the figures that he quoted in his various letters.

The strong possibility of promotion must have acted as a powerful incentive to many new entrants. Certainly an officer could expect to become a supervisor at least with the very outside chance of making a collector's post. Promotion in the service was based solely on merit and patronage had very little effect. Any officer of only moderate ability, providing he showed some sense of urgency and avoided too much drink, could hope to be promoted to supervisor within nine years. Burns, had he lived, would have been appointed supervisor in a little over seven years.

As if the salary and promotion prospects were not sufficient inducements for new entrants, all the Scottish Excise posts were pensionable. That is not to say that there was a set retirement age, indeed was there any *legal* entitlement to a pension. Officers applied to the Excise Board for permission to retire and at the same time for a grant of a pension. Each application was considered by the Commissioners on its merits. The length of service (minimum seven years), the character of the applicant during his career and the reason for retirement were all carefully weighed before a sum was decided. Supervisors received no more than £20 per year and officers from £8 to £16. During most of the eighteenth century few officers applied for a pension; in 1794 there were only twenty-eight on the 'Charitie Fund'. As there was no upper age bar most officers worked on and died in harness. However, the arduous nature of the work is shown by the fact that few serving officers survived beyond the age of sixty. An exception was a Thomas Vaughan, a supervisor at Lanark, who was seventy-four years old and shown as 'very active but insane'! It was not until the early years of the nineteenth century that the Charity Fund was transformed into a legal superannuation fund with contributions of 2½% of salary and larger pensions awarded. James Graham, a colleague of Burns at Dumfries, retired in 1810 on health grounds at the age of forty-eight with a pension of £32 a year and he survived for another twenty-four years so he did very well out the Excise Board.

Considering that most officers died in post, more important was the provision of a pension fund for officers' widows and orphans. The scheme, which was quite unique, went under the exalted title of 'The Excise Incorporation of Scotland' and had been first introduced in 1748. The scheme was divided into three classes—collectors and equivalent ranks, supervisors, and lastly officers. Robert Burns paid 8s per quarter plus 6d 'for expenses' and as a result his widow Jean Armour received an annual payment of £8 until 1821 when it was increased to £12, a sum she received until her death in 1834. Admittedly the annuity was not a great fortune but the intention of the Fund was purely to prevent the destitution of an officer's family in the eventuality of his early death. This Scottish Excise scheme was in advance of the times and several decades would pass before a similar fund was established in England.

It is perhaps now clearer why a post in the Excise was such an attractive proposition. A position that offered certain and steady work, a regular income, the chances of extra payments, promotion prospects and the security of a pension for one's self and family, was so very rare in the eighteenth century. Surely under such conditions of employment the 'Ignominy of the Excise' could be better tolerated, if not almost forgotten?

EXCISE DOCUMENT SHOWING OFFICERS SERVING IN DUMFRIES DISTRICT, 1791.
(HMSO).

Chapter Three

The year 1786 must be viewed as the *annus mirabilis* as far as Robert Burns's fortunes were concerned, although at the time he would not have recognised it as such. Nevertheless, at the age of twenty-seven, he stood at the threshold of his greatest achievements. On 31st July the publication of the Kilmarnock Poems turned him, almost overnight, from a mere Ayrshire farmer into a national poet–the unofficial laureate of Scotland. The 'heaven-taught Ploughman' had been discovered and 'his native genius' recognised. Then, in November, began the long, valuable and valued friendship with Mrs. Dunlop, which was to last almost the rest of his life. In the following month he first captivated and then triumphantly conquered Edinburgh society. By then some of the mental torture endured at the hands of the Armour family, the depression and misery which led to thoughts of emigration to Jamaica, and the deep sorrow at the death of Mary Campbell, 'Highland Mary', had been somewhat dissipated.

It was also in this year that it can be said with certainty that he was considering the possibilities of an Excise career. In October he wrote a long and revealing letter to Robert Aiken, in which he expressed a feeling of;

..all the various notations and movements within, respecting the
excise. There are many things plead strongly against it; the
uncertainty of getting soon into business, the consequences of my
follies, which may perhaps make it impracticable for me to stay at
home.

(C. L. p. 93)

Not a very enthusiastic response, but the letter does imply that a plan to enter the Excise had been under discussion previously and it is quite likely that Aiken had first floated the idea.

Aiken was a writer (lawyer) in Ayr and had first met Burns in 1783. He was the first person, outside the poet's immediate circle of friends, to recognise the merits of Burns's poetry and was most active in helping him with the Kilmarnock edition–Burns considered him 'My first kind patron'. Aiken, the son of a sea-captain, was a writer of some repute and was very well-connected in Ayr and he would surely have known John Wright, the Excise Collector, who had been based in the town since 1773. Unfortunately much of Burns's correspondence with Aiken was destroyed so Aiken's part, if any, in the poet's choice of a future career can never be established.

Burns however, was very likely to have a fair idea of the Excise and an officer's duties already. After all, there were Excise officers stationed in Mauchline and Tarbolton and in such small and closed communities–in 1971 the population of Mauchline was only 1,000 persons–the Excise gauger would be a well-known figure to most, if not all. It is even more likely that Burns would have met an officer in one of the several taverns he frequented–the occupational hazard of eighteenth century Excise life was drink! Perhaps Burns had even witnessed the officer inspecting the entry book of the local publican and watched him check the stocks of spirits before mounting his horse to ride off to another tavern to repeat his duties or to survey some distant malthouse.

The attraction of such a life, riding around the Scottish countryside observing nature and the change of seasons with, apparently, all the time in the world to think about life and his poetry, such freedom would no doubt have appealed to Burns's restless spirit. The hardships and confines of farming life with its uncertain reward compared unfavourably with the independence of the gauger's life. The security of the salary of £50 would have seemed a veritable fortune when contrasted with £7 a year that he and his brother had drawn for their unremitting labours–not for nothing did he liken himself to 'a galley slave'.

Perhaps, much to his surprise, he had discovered that his formal education–albeit rather sporadic and fragmentary–would indeed stand him in good stead if ever he attempted to secure an Excise post. Besides a basic schooling in English grammar and some French at the hands of John Murdoch, his father had tutored him in simple arithmetic. He had also attended a school in Dalrymple, a small village a few miles from Ayr, in the summer of 1773 to improve his handwriting. This was not wasted, even if one ignores the numbers of letters he wrote, because one of the main qualifications for entry into the Excise was 'to write a good hand'.

More important for his future career was the summer he spent two years later, when he left Alloway to stay with his maternal uncle at Kirkoswald, situated near the coast some ten miles south of Ayr. It was here that the local schoolmaster, Hugh Rodger, had established a fine reputation as a teacher of mathematics. Burns had been sent there to learn, 'mensuration, surveying, dialling and etc...' Although the object of this instruction was to help the laying-out and planning of the new farm at Lochlea, the 'pretty good progress' that he made proved to be of great value in his later life.

No person could enter the Excise service without understanding 'the first four rules of Vulgar and Decimal Arithematic' [sic]. The *Royal Gauger,* the vademecum of Excise practice, demanded a reasonably high standard of numerical knowledge and skill. The book described in detail the use of square and cube roots, the intricate methods of gauging casks and other utensils, the use of a sliding rule to ascertain the capabilities and ullages of casks and 'decimal fractions'–all the required expertise so essential to an officer's day-to-day work. Without a previous grounding in mathematics a new entrant into the Excise would find the work most difficult despite the period of instruction.

That Burns had received instruction in such subjects was fairly unusual in the eighteenth century. The most vaunted public schools of the time, let alone the lesser private schools, hardly touched upon mathematics and science; their curricula were based almost entirely on the classics. Even in the following century many students left these schools without a good knowledge of English, let alone mathematics, and some could barely write. So although Burns's father had other reasons for sending his bright son to Kirkoswald he did in fact do him a good service as it turned out in the long run. The image of the 'self-taught ploughman' is not strictly true.

It was not only in numerical knowledge that the young man gained during his short stay at Kirkoswald as he explained in his famous autobiographical letter to Dr. Moore;

> ...But I made greater progress in the knowledge of mankind. The contraband trade was at that time very successful; scenes of swaggering riot and roaring dissipation were as yet new to me; and I was no enemy to social life.

(C.L.p.248-256)

The whole of the coast was notorious for its smuggling. One parish minister suggested that 'the inhabitants of Kirkoswald owing to the prevalence of smuggling attained a measure of refinement in the manner of living and dress earlier than in the neighbouring parishes.' Certainly most of the farmers kept boats, ostensibly for fishing, but the majority were used solely for the smuggling trade. Douglas Graham of Shanter called his smuggling boat *Tam O' Shanter* –the name immortalised in the famous narrative poem.

By the time of Burns's visit an incident known as the 'Battle of Howshean Moor' had passed into smuggling folk-lore. It related to a particularly violent and bloody affray between a party of smugglers that was ambushed by revenue officers; both sides were armed and suffered many casualties with one fatality. This story and other similar tales must have excited the impressionable young man, who had hitherto hardly ventured far from the quiet backwater of Alloway. Although he subsequently admitted that his 'Trigonometry...and Sines' (C.L.p.253), had suffered as the result of a certain young lady, who lived next door to the school, the experiences he gained at Kirkoswald must not be underestimated in the light of his later career.

The six months that Burns spent in Irvine in 1781 learning the trade of a flax-heckler influenced him in many ways. Not least was his re-introduction into the smuggling world. The Royal Burgh of Irvine was still one of the most important ports in Scotland though its trade was fast disappearing to the newly established port on the Clyde–Port Glasgow. The town had a lively and cosmopolitan society and was the centre of the smuggling trade in north Ayrshire. There was a plentiful supply of the strong but harsh spirit from the many illicit stills in the area and the best 'Nantz'–the duty-free French brandy–could be easily obtained at the numerous taverns that crowded the old port. From his experiences in Irvine Burns could never complain that he did not know what revenue work entailed.

Perhaps at this stage of his life Burns might have sympathised with the free-trade ethos. Two years later in July 1783 he wrote in a letter to his cousin James Burness in Montrose;

> ..There is a great trade of smuggling carried along our coasts, which, however destructive to the interests of the kingdom at large, certainly enriches this corner of it; but too often indeed at the expense of our morals: however, it enables individuals to make, at least for a time, a splendid appearance.

(C.L.p.58)

Some ambivalence towards the smuggling fraternity can be detected here. In a letter of 4th May 1788 to Samuel Brown, his uncle at Kirkoswald;

>...I engaged in the smuggling trade and God knows if ever any poor
>man experienced better returns–two for one–But as freight and
>Delivery has turned out so D..mnd Dear I am thinking of taking out a
>Licence and beginning in the fair trade.

(C.L.p.451)

Burns, in this letter, was merely using the smuggling trade as a colourful simile for his illicit relationship with Jean Armour; the reference to 'taking out a Licence and beginning in the fair trade', meant that he was thinking of marrying Jean. Burns was probably well aware that his uncle dabbled in smuggling and felt that he would appreciate such news disguised in 'free-trade' terms.

Although Samuel Brown would no doubt have appreciated the joke, it was most unwise of Burns to write such comments considering he was virtually in the middle of his Excise training at the time. He would have had considerable difficulty in explaining away such a letter should it have fallen into the wrong hands. One of the cardinal rules of the smuggling trade was that nothing was imparted to paper. Although there is evidence that he had some sympathy with the smugglers (indeed most eighteenth century people, did even including Adam Smith) there is absolutely no evidence that he ever engaged in the trade.

It has been suggested that Burns had a secondary aim in mind when he set out for Edinburgh on 27th November 1786. The main reason for the journey, and in my view the only one, was to arrange for a second edition of his *Poems*. The only evidence that an Excise post was under consideration comes in a letter he received from Sir John Whitefoord in early December 1786. Sir John had previously lived at Ballochmyle, barely two miles south of Mauchline, until 1788 when he was forced to sell his estate and move to Edinburgh. His first contact with Burns must have dated from 1781 when Burns was initiated into St. James Masonic Lodge at Tarbolton, where Sir John was the Master of the Lodge; and a closer association arose after the poet was appointed Depute Master in 1784.

Within days of arriving in Edinburgh Burns sought the interest of Sir John. The reply from Sir John mentioned 'your wish to be made a gauger'. This most likely refers to Burns's thoughts and misgivings on the subject back in the autumn. Although Sir John felt that 'your character as a man as well as a poet entitles you, I think, to the assistance of every inhabitant of Ayrshire', he advised Burns that any money raised by subscription for the second edition should be laid out on the stocking of a small farm. It was not really the answer that Burns was looking for, but subsequently he took the advice.

Nevertheless, Sir John proved to be a steady and true friend and he was instrumental in introducing Burns into the Canongate Kilwinning Lodge in Edinburgh, among whose members were the Earl of Glencairn, Lord Torphicen, Lord Elcho, the lawyer Alexander Cunningham, the schoolmaster William Nicol, the publisher William Creech, and the painter Alexander Nasmyth, all of whom figured largely in the poet's life in the capital. It was strongly rumoured (though never proven) that freemasonry was flourishing in the English Excise and had an undue influence upon appointments and promotions; whether this applied to the Scottish Excise is not known but Burns's masonic brethren were certainly a help to him.

It seems very likely that Burns took Sir John's advice to heart and by March 1787 he informed Mrs. Dunlop that he intended 'to return to my old acquaintance the plough' (C.L.p.135). There is no further mention of the Excise for almost a year. Furthermore, the rather dilatory manner in which he acted on Mrs. Dunlop's introduction to Adam Smith, as described earlier, suggests that Burns had put aside all thoughts of any Government appointment.

The summer and autumn of 1787 turned out to be one of the happiest periods of Burns's life. He had been fêted and lionised by Edinburgh society and had achieved his main objective when, in April, a second and much enlarged edition of his Poems was published. The first Edinburgh edition was sold by subscription arranged through leading members of the Caledonian Hunt, an association of noblemen and country gentlemen of which both Glencairn and Sir John were members. Burns was enrolled as a member in April 1792–a sure sign that he had finally 'arrived'. The first edition was re-set almost immediately as it had been greatly oversubscribed, and in the end three thousand copies in all were published–quite amazing figures. On 23rd April, just two days after publication, Burns sold the copyright to Creech, his publisher, for £100. It is estimated (though figures vary) that Burns cleared over £800 from the edition, though it is unfortunate that Creech proved very tardy in settling the account.

With some money in his pocket, and being financially secure for the first time in his life, Burns now felt the urge to see something of Scotland beyond the capital and his native Ayrshire. The object of the various tours he undertook during May to October was;

> ...to make leisurely pilgrimages through Caledonia; to sit on the
> fields of her battles, to wander on the romantic banks of her rivers;
> and to muse by the stately towers of venerable ruins, once the
> honoured abode of her heroes.
>
> (C.L.p.134)

It was during his second Highland tour that Burns met Robert Graham, the newly appointed Excise Commissioner, who was destined to have such an influential effect on his future life. If Burns had stayed at Blair Atholl longer than the two days, as he was earnestly requested to, he would have met Henry Dundas, the most powerful man in Scotland, who was due at the Castle the following day. Such a meeting might have made some difference to his career. On the other hand, there is evidence to suggest that Dundas was afraid of the outspoken young poem, especially as the tide of radicalism began to rise.

Dundas, Member of Parliament for Midlothian from 1774 to 1790, held several high offices in the Pitt administration, being successively Lord Advocate (1775) Treasurer of the Navy (1782) and Home Secretary (1791), and was created Viscount Melville in 1801. As Government election agent, he controlled the election of nearly all the Scottish members of the House of Commons and wielded so much power in Scotland for thirty years that he was virtually the uncrowned 'King of Scotland'. There is no doubt that if he had wished to take an interest in Burns, he could have obtained for him a Government post. However, it is unlikely that he could have improved on the Excise position finally obtained by Burns despite all his influence; instead perhaps Dundas could have found Burns a more 'comfortable' situation in one of the other revenue services–Posts, Stamps or even Customs, though in the latter department Burns had not actively pursued his introduction to Smith. It has been suggested that Dundas may even have engineered Burns's appointment, if only to curb him and the better to have his words and deeds closely monitored.

Burns was back in Edinburgh in October 1787 and he was forced seriously to consider his future. The success and euphoria of his first visit had somewhat died away, he had tired of Edinburgh and the countryside beckoned him. The offer of a farm on the Dalswinton estate in the valley of the Nith at Dumfries had been first proposed by Patrick Miller as far back as January. Burns realised that he could prevaricate no longer; a decision must be made–accept or reject it. Whether he had any further thoughts on the Excise at that time is not recorded, but he had planned to leave Edinburgh in early December without apparently making any further moves on the subject, though this is not certain because he had been making frequent visits to William Nimmo's sister was the attraction. A more plausible explanation would appear to be that he was seeking ways to forward a petition to the Excise Board. Nimmo was a supervisor of long seniority and was well-known and well-connected at Head Office. It was, of course, at a fateful tea-party hosted by Nimmo's sister, Erskine, that Burns met Mrs. Agnes McLehose–Clarinda–and fate played another hand with Burns's unfortunate accident, which kept him in Edinburgh far longer than he had planned.

Lockhart, however, in his biography of Burns published in 1828, states that Alexander Wood (or 'Lang Sandy' as he was known), the surgeon who attended Burns when he injured his knee in a fall from a coach, heard of his patient's dilemma over the Excise and went directly to Robert Graham to petition on behalf of his patient. The truth of this statement cannot be verified, but it does not seem very likely as it was not in accord with the normal procedure even as far as patronage was concerned.

What is known as fact, is that Burns wrote to Robert Graham on 7th January 1788 reminding him of their previous meeting at 'Atholehouse' and begging his patronage 'in this affair' (C.L.p.424). It is also obvious from the letter that Burns had already submitted an application to the Excise Board and had also obtained the necessary certificate signed by a supervisor. This would imply that Burns had either acted on Nimmo's advice or perhaps been guided by Adam Pearson, the Excise Secretary and Nimmo's close friend, on the correct and proper procedure. It would have been quite possible for him to be appointed without personally involving a Commissioner. Both Nimmo and Pearson had sufficient influence and Burns's fame in the country would have ensured a sympathetic hearing; the support of Robert Graham merely ensured that he would be accepted.

But suddenly things went sadly amiss. On 27th January Burns wrote to Clarinda;

> ...I have almost given up the excise idea..I have been just now to
> wait on a great person..I have been questioned like a child about my
> matters and blamed and schooled for my inscription on Stirling
> window.

(C.L.p.390)

The 'great person' was most likely to be Thomas Wharton. Wharton acted as the unofficial Chairman of the Excise Board, as befitted the only Treasury appointee.

He had previously served as the Deputy Solicitor of the English Excise and for good measure had married the daughter of the Earl of Fife–no doubt a 'great person' in Burns's eyes. Some writers have suggested that Burns was told to put his personal affairs in order before he could join the Excise–hence his 'acknowledgement' of Jean Armour as his wife, which was confirmed by the Mauchline Kirk on 5th August. This view seems completely wrong not only because he instructed Jean Armour to keep silent on the matter but it would be most unlikely for the Excise Board to demand such from Burns. Eighteenth century Excise officers were not well-known for their morality, and both Boards seemed to accept 'wenching', judging by some of their comments on officers. I feel that Burns was merely warned about his future conduct as an Excise officer.

The greater concern to the Board and I suspect to Wharton, in particular, was the Jacobite inscription scratched on the Stirling tavern window. The ten lines refer to 'The injur'd Stewart-line' being gone and replaced by–

An idiot race, to honour lost–
Who know them best despise them most.

Written by Somebody on the Window (C.W.p.286)

Such outright Jacobite sentiments the Board could not tolerate nor indeed condone. Burns was seriously concerned that his Excise application would be refused and therefore he wrote to the Earl of Glencairn to elicit his support for his application. It seems more than a coincidence that the letter to Glencairn was postmarked 1st February–just a few days after the painful interview. In any case he probably thought that two 'friends at court' were better than one!

In just over a fortnight matters had so improved he was able to inform Margaret Chalmers, the charming young lady who had so captivated Burns that he proposed marriage only to be politely refused, that;

...I have entered into the Excise and will be in the west for three weeks and then return to Edinburgh for six weeks instruction...the commissioners are some of them my acquaintances and all of them my firm friends.

(C.L.p.236)

–quite a change in such a short time! He left Edinburgh in late February to resolve the question of the farm but quite convinced in his own mind that 'the Excise must be my lot.'

Attempting to trace Burns's steps during the next six weeks is like chasing a will of the wisp. It proved to be the most hectic period of his life and he finally made decisions that virtually decided the pattern of the rest of his life. He set off from Edinburgh on 18th February and made for Glasgow, where he undertook 'a commission' for a friend, and met his sea-captain friend from his Irvine days as well as seeing his younger brother. From there he went to Paisley and Kilmarnock before arriving at Tarbolton. It was here that Jean Armour was staying at the house of his friends–the Muirs. Within days he had found a room for Jean at Mauchline and provided a bed just in time for her to produce twins for the second time (both died within a few weeks). Whilst he alleviated his brother's financial problems and managed to make some headway in healing the breach in his relations with the Armour family.

By the end of February he was back on the road again, this time to Dumfries to inspect the farm at Ellisland with John Tennant, his farming 'expert'. This visit was purely out of 'politeness to Patrick Miller', so utterly convinced was Burns that the Excise was his only solution. On 2nd March he stayed at Cumnock on his way back to Mauchline and Mossgiel. Burns was back in Edinburgh on 19th March where he sought some financial settlement with Creech, his publisher, and three days later he signed the lease of the farm–Tennant had convinced him of its worth against Burns's better judgment. On 19th March he went 'to sup among some of the principals of the Excise' and on the following evening he 'dined with one of the commissioners'–Robert Graham perhaps? But Burns was now secure in the knowledge that he had his 'order for instructions' safely tucked in his pocket.

By 21st March he had left Edinburgh for Mauchline, where he divided his time between 'his wife', as he now called her, and his brother's farm. There were several visits to Ayr in the intervening period, mainly I feel to re-arrange his Excise instruction. At a very conservative estimate he must have travelled over 500 miles in he previous weeks in winter conditions and yet he still managed to find time to write a mass of letters. As he put it, 'I have fought my way severely through the savage hospitality of this country to send every guest drunk to bed' (C.L.p.359). Small wonder then that he complained that 'his unlucky knee..will scarcely stand the fatigue of my Excise instruction.'

The next stage in furthering his Excise cause was to undertake the six weeks formal training at the hands of a suitable officer. It is quite clear that he had originally intended this instruction to take place in Edinburgh. The normal procedure for an aspiring Excise candidate was to find an officer willing to instruct him, then obtain the approval of the officer's supervisor and finally agree the fees to be paid–in the majority of cases these were £2 for the officer and £1 for the supervisor, half on commencement and the balance on completion of training. It was not until 1870 that Excise officers received free tuition. The candidate was required to obtain their agreement in writing and submit it to the Excise Board, who would issue a formal order for instruction if they considered the officer as 'a fit person to instruct'.

Burns's original choice of instructor was Alexander Dickson, an officer in Edinburgh of some twelve years service who was thought by the Board to be 'a good sober officer'–indeed he was promoted to supervisor in June 1788. Possibly because of his somewhat tangled and difficult private affairs Burns felt that it might be better to be away from Edinburgh and the attractions of Clarinda and closer to Mauchline and his new 'wife'. He therefore arranged to be instructed by the officer at Tarbolton, some six miles from Mauchline.

However, a slight complication now arose. The supervisor at Ayr, George Johnston, would not accept the instruction order, which named Dickson despite the fact that the order had to be re-assigned to the officer at Tarbolton. Johnston was, according to Burns, 'superstitiously strict' and so Burns had no alternative but to ask Robert Graham to intervene in the matter. He wrote from Mauchline on 25th March and explained his dilemma; it was an earnest appeal to Graham to use his influence to obtain a new instruction order. Time was also vitally important as Burns had signed to take over the farm at Whitsuntime (which was the end of May). Burns said in his letter to Graham that the new instructing officer was 'exceedingly clever and who enters with the warmth of a friend in my ideas of being instructed' (C.L.p.425).

The officer in question was James Findlay, a single man with seven years experience and at thirty-one was only two years older than Burns. The Board thought highly of him, as an 'active good officer'. It is possible that Burns was already acquainted with Findlay. He may have been a member of the Tarbolton Bachelors Club, which Burns and his brother had started back in 1781. Nevertheless, there was an affinity between them in the light of Burns's comment, 'the warmth of a friend'.

Graham acted swiftly and the order for instruction was dated 31st March and signed by Adam Pearson. It is worth repeating the order in full to show how comprehensive the Excise training was;

> That you instruct the bearer, Robert Burns, in the art of gauging and
> practical dry gouging casks and utensils; and that you fit him for
> surveying victuallers, rectifiers, chandlers, tanners, tawers,
> maltsters etc; and when he has kept books regularly for six weeks at
> least, and drawn true vouchers and abstracts therefrom (which
> books, vouchers and abstracts must be signed by your supervisor
> and yourself, as well as the said Robert Burns) and sent to the
> Commissioners at his expense; and when he is furnished with
> proper instruments, and well instructed and qualified for an officer,
> then (and not before, at your perils) you and your supervisor are to
> certify the same to the Board, expressing particularly therein the
> date of this letter; and that the above Robert Burns hath cleared his
> quarters, both for lodging and diet; that he has actually paid each of
> you for his instruction and examination and that he has sufficient at
> the time to purchase a horse for his business.

The period of instruction started in the middle of April and on the 28th of the month Burns decided to inform his friend Mrs. Dunlop about his new situation;

> ...As I got the offer of the Excise business without solicitation to
> entitle me to a Commission; which Commission lies by me and at any
> future period on my simple petition can be resumed; I thought five
> and thirty pounds a year was no bad dernier resort for a poor Poet, if
> fortune in her jade tricks should kick him down from the little
> eminence to which she has lately helped him up–For this reason I am
> at present attending these instructions to have them completed by
> Whitsunday.

(C.L.p.144)

It is interesting to note that Burns considered that he had obtained his Excise nomination 'without solicitation'. Was this a bit of bluff on his behalf and had he conveniently forgotten the letters to· Graham and Glencairn? Perhaps it adds further credence to my view that the decision had already been made irrespective of Graham's interest.

His instructions were duly completed by the end of May though it would appear that he had found them 'a bit of a plague'. However, he was obviously a quick and ready pupil because six weeks was the *minimum* time allowed, often the period was extended if the candidate was slow to pick up the intricacies of gauging and Excise accounting. The examination at the hands of the supervisor was certainly not a perfunctory check. Johnston would have accompanied Burns on visits to brewers, maltsters and victuallers and watched whilst he took gauges and dips and then completed the necessary books, accounts and vouchers to his complete satisfaction; it must be remembered that Johnston had a reputation for being punctilious.

Whether Burns had to obtain the necessary implements of his trade, though he was not intending entering the Excise immediately, is not known; but eventually he would have to purchase, *at least,* a gauging stick and sliding cane, both used for measuring beer cisterns, vats and coopers, a sliding rule for gauging small casks and calculating quantities and ullages, and a box and tape used for measuring gauges of malt, as well as a brass plate and cork float used for malt and beer dipping. In addition, a new officer would be expected to provide himself with a practical book on gauging and Excise procedure, and a digest of Excise laws was quite essential. Therefore, it can be seen that the expense incurred in setting oneself up as an Excise officer was not extra inconsiderable.

On 11th June 1788 Burns started farming at Ellisland, though the Excise was not far from his thoughts. He wrote to Aiken, 'As it is. I look to the excise scheme as a certainty of maintenance...' And just over a month later he had his Excise Commission 'in his pocket'. The Commission had been signed on 14th July 1788 by three Commissioners–Thomas Wharton, George Brown and James Stoddard–it was strange that Graham was not one of the signatories. Burns was now a fully qualified Excise officer and could take up any post that was offered. In the normal course of events he would have been termed an 'expectant', in other words having to wait for a vacancy to arise. Indeed further evidence that he was placed 'on the books of the Excise' was the entry under his name in the Register of Official Characters, which showed, 'Never tryed; a Poet' and a different hand added later 'Turns out well'. It is interesting to note that Burns's Excise commission was sold in London in 1854 for a mere £5 12s. 0d; it surfaced again in London in 1923 for £550. What would its price be now?

In August 1788 Burns confided to Mrs. Dunlop that he intended to write to Robert Graham;

> ...on whose friendship my Excise hopes depend...one of the
> worthiest and most accomplished Gentleman, not only of this
> Country, but I will dare say it, of this Age.

(C.L.p.151)

The letter had been 'long thought out' and was finally written on 10th September and with it Burns enclosed a poem dedicated to Graham, 'When Nature her great Masterpiece designed'. The letter set forward a proposal which Burns must have been considering for some time.

Although Burns felt that the farm would ultimately be 'a saving bargain' it was not yet 'such a Pennyworth as I was taught to expect' (C.L.p.426). His solution to his financial problems was a scheme to combine farming and the Excise. It was this plan, and perhaps the boldness with which he proposed it, that gave rise to strong criticism by subsequent biographers. Put in the simplest terms Burns asked whether Graham could arrange to remove the officer in whose area Ellisland was situated and appoint him to the post. Burns excused himself by explaining that the officer in question, who also rented a farm near Ellisland, was 'quite opulent' and such a removal would cause him little inconvenience.

The officer who was to be moved to accommodate Burns was Leonard Smith. Smith had been in the Service some nine years, the last three of them at Dumfries. It was certainly true that he was opulent, having a fortune derived from the estate of his wife's mother. Furthermore, the Excise Board did not rate him very highly, Smith's official character read, 'Pretty good, drinks', though Burns would not have been aware of this. It is possible that it was common knowledge that Smith showed a lack of urgency and interest in his Excise business but at this time there is no evidence that Burns knew any of the Dumfries officers. Smith's subsequent Excise career was rather chequered. He was suspended in 1790 but re-instated only to be suspended once again in 1796. He was never again re-employed although he twice petitioned for a post; these appeals for re-employment do not suggest a lack of interest in the Excise on his behalf.

So how justified is the criticism of Burns in this matter? His action certainly shows an unscrupulous side to Burns's character although he later admitted that;

> I could not bear to injure a poor fellow by ousting him to make way
> for myself; to the wealthy son of good-fortune like Smith, the injury
> is imaginary where the propriety of your rules admits.

(C.L.p.427)

In mitigation it must be borne in mind that Excise officers *expected* to be moved every four to five years: it was official policy not to keep officers too long in one place in order to prevent over-familiarity with the Excise traders, which, in the Board's view, 'might endanger the Revenue'. The unpopularity of 'removes' as far as the officers were concerned was the expense involved, which they had to bear themselves, and in Smith's case this would be minimal because of his financial situation and the fact that, at the time, he had no family. I consider the criticism is a little unfair considering Burns was living in an age when patronage was all important and it would have been foolish and rather short-sighted of him not to have made use of the valuable contact he had in Graham. Also at the time Burns thought that he could combine farming and the Excise and Smith's station was the only one in the area where he could hope to do the two jobs. Burns's abiding concern was providing for his growing family and he was prepared to use any avenue at his command to achieve some security for his wife and children.

Graham, however, informed him that he did not have the power to arrange such a move, as there were certain regulations in force which prevented even a Commissioner taking such a decision. Burns's future in the Excise, if he wished to remain in Dumfries, rested solely in the hands of the Collector at Dumfries; only he had the power to move officers within his collection or recommend to the Excise Board that an officer should be move out of his collection. Graham wrote a letter of introduction for Burns and in May 1789 Burns met his future Collector, John Mitchell, for the first time.

Mitchell had originally intended going into the ministry but instead joined the Excise in 1751; he had served as officer and supervisor in many parts of Scotland, latterly as supervisor at Wigtown, and had only been promoted to Collector at Dumfries in 1788. He was said to be a kind and benevolent man and a competent official, though the Board thought him 'just middling'. He was certainly not sympathetic to Burns, who later called him 'Friend of the Poet, tried and leal'. By

THE "CHARACTER" OF BURNS FROM EXCISE RECORDS 1792. (*HMSO*).

the end of July Burns was able to report back to Graham that Mitchell could see that the removal of Leonard Smith 'will be productive of at least no disadvantage to the Revenue and may likewise be done without any detriment to him.' Burns was now almost there; it only remained for the Excise Board to approve his appointment after Smith had been moved. Perhaps what tilted the balance was 'the sharp reprimand' Smith received in 1789 from the Board for some misdemeanour, which gave the Collector an excuse to request Smith's removal.

Burns was now so confident that his appointment was imminent that he started to study his Excise instructions and Leadbetter's *Royal Gauger* as well as working at 'Breman's rule'–this was a four-foot gauging rod devised by Breman, an Excise collector, which also served as a slide rule. It was actually cleverly jointed and folded down to one foot for ease of carrying; the rule was universally used in both the English and Scottish Excise. A very delighted Burns was able to tell Mrs. Dunlop in the middle of August;

> ...I have been once more a lucky fellow in that quarter [the Excise].
> The Exciseman's Salaries are now £50 per ann and I believe the
> Board have been so obliging as to fix me in the Division in which I
> live; and I suppose I shall begin in doing duty at the commencement
> of next month. I shall have a large portion of country but what to me
> and my studies is no trifling matter, it is fine romantic country.
>
> (C.L.p.177)

The precise date of Burns's entry into the Excise is, unfortunately, not known but it seems most likely that he started on his official career in the first week of September 1789. Before he could take up his appointment, however, there were a few legal formalities to be completed. There were two oaths to swear and he had to obtain a certificate, signed by a Minister and witnesses, that he had received 'the sacrament according to the usage of the Church of Scotland'.

Two oaths, one of allegiance and one of office, were required to be taken before a Court of Exchequer; though in Scotland Excise collectors had been delegated this task and I have no doubt that they treated it with due solemnity. Burns had to declare that he would 'sincerely bear true allegiance and be faithful to King George III'. The oath of office laid emphasis on the execution of his office 'truly and faithfully without favour and affection' and also that he would not take any fee or reward in his Excise post. The Communion certificate was most likely to have been given by the Rev. Joseph Kirkpatrick, the Minister of Dunscore parish wherein Ellisland was situated. It is known that Burns attended the church though he found Kirkpatrick 'one vast constellation of dullness'!

There was one further oath to be sworn–that of 'Abjuration'. This had to be subscribed at the next Quarter Sessions following his entry into the Service. Burns attended the Dumfries Quarter Sessions on 27th October for this purpose. The oath required him 'to acknowledge, profess, testify and declare in his conscience and before God and the World that King George III was the lawful and rightful King and that he would continually bear faith to His Majesty.' But that was not all, for he had to swear further that he would defend him against 'all traitorous Conspiracies and attempts, which shall be made against his person.' It can now be understood more clearly why any adverse words or deeds against the Monarchy were treated so seriously by the Excise Board. Burns was compelled to keep this certificate of oath with him at all times, as he could be asked to produce it by a superior officer at will.

Thus, at long last, Burns became an Excise officer almost eighteen months after his spell of instruction. This long delay was most unusual and one wonders just how much knowledge of the art of gauging he had managed to retain. N.P.[Burns's first Excise station was known as Dumfries First Itinerary, or more commonly a 'ride' or 'out-ride'. Dumfries district comprised twelve stations. The town itself was divided into three divisions, one of which had the responsibility of the port. Bridgend, another footwalk division, was situated on the west bank of the Nith, just outside the Royal Burgh on the main road to Newton Stewart. There were three itineraries to cover the country surrounding Dumfries. The first was roughly situated to the north and north west of the burgh and the other two ran due south of the town divided by the Nith as it flowed into the Solway. Much farther afield there were itineraries at Sanquhar, Lochmaben, Lockerbie, Annan and Woodhouse. It was a very widespread district under the control of a supervisor, who was based in Dumfries, as was the collector.

Burns said of his Excise area that it was so extensive that he had 'no less than ten parishes to ride over' and that it 'so abounded with business' that he could 'scarce steal a moment' (C.L.p.422). He later explained that he was in the saddle for five, or at least four, days in the week, often riding thirty to forty miles a day and sometimes he covered two hundred miles in a week. This is no exaggeration on his part as all Excise stations were schemed on a fortnightly basis and officers were only allowed one rest day in fourteen (Sundays, of course, excepted).

Unfortunately there are no surviving Excise records or maps to show the exact extent of the various Excise areas. It is possible, however, by careful interpretation of the existing Excise records relating to Burns, to build up a fairly accurate picture of Dumfries First Itinerary. As all Excise stations, both in England and Scotland, were based on parishes, it can be assumed that his station would be linked to the parish boundaries and, of course, to the shire boundary. In addition, the two other main sources of information for the picture are Findlater's diary of June/July 1792 when he inspected Burns's old station (Burns was then in Dumfries) and a similar record by Burns written in December 1794 when he inspected his old station as acting supervisor during Findlater's illnesses. Each report records the places actually visited in the area and by allying these details to Burns's 'ten parishes' an approximate map can be drawn.

The ten parishes were Durisdeer, Morton, Closeburn, Holywood, Dunscore, Glencairn, Tynron, Keir, Penpont and Kirkmahoe. As Burns had been at pains to point out to Robert Graham, his farm was right in the middle of an Excise station and certainly Ellisland could hardly have been better placed for his Excise work.

To delineate Burns's Excise area, one must travel due south from Ellisland almost to Dumfries, then across the Nith to follow the road along the east bank of the river passing through Dalswinton (Patrick Miller's estate), Aldgirth (now known as Auldgirth), Brownhill and Thornhill to Carronbridge. Here the road divided, one branch going north-west to Sanquhar. Burns, however, would have to take the route to the north-east, which was the old Roman road, and led to Durisdeer and past to Muircleugh on the edge of the Lowther Hills, the most northerly extremity of his ride. He then had to retrace his steps back to Carronbridge and cross the Nith to follow the New Galloway road which passed through Penpont, Tynron, Minihive (Moniaive) as far as Achenchain (Auchencheyne) virtually on the border between Kirkcudbrightshire and Dumfriesshire. This boundary would form the western and southern limits of his station, which encompassed the Nith valley and such places as Kirkland, Keir and Dunscore.

From Excise documents we know that Burns's station consisted of five separate rides, which covered 170 miles. As such, it was by far the largest area in the Dumfries district; quite a daunting task for a fledgling officer. Burns was compelled to survey one full ride each day and he was enjoined not to do so in 'any constant way' or indeed in any set pattern and certainly not to start at the same place each day. The pattern of his control was to be irregular, making his visits at the most unexpected times. Moreover, he should not be too often in the rides nearest to Ellisland but to inspect the more remote parts of his area more frequently. Frequently he would be expected to make a return visit to a place that he had visited earlier in the same day: the element of surprise was to be his watchword. One of the cardinal rules of Excise control was the avoidance of regular habits. Considering that it was something in excess of twenty miles from Ellisland to the most distant point of his ride, it is not really surprising that he spent so many hours riding and covering such long distances each day. One can only sympathise with Burns when he wrote of 'some injuries in a part that shall be nameless owing to a hard-hearted stone of a saddle'! (C.L.p.563). Another fact to be borne in mind is that during the winter months many of the roads to the north and west of his area, which were especially hilly, would be almost impassable. N.P.[Indeed, Burns recounts a journey as acting supervisor in December 1794 when he had to struggle through ten-foot snowdrifts on the road to Lochmaben. He was very proud of the fact that he still managed to get through to the town despite the inclement weather. It was not until the Turnpike Acts of the 1790s that some of the roads in the area were improved, largely funded by tolls; but by this time Burns was settled in the relative comfort and ease of a foot-walk division in Dumfries.

The Excise duties in force in Scotland at the time were on beer, malt, tea, salt, tobacco, soap, candles, glass, bricks, calicoes, paper, leather, and of course, spirits. The total amount collected in 1790 was £419,500 and over half this amount came from beer, malt and spirits. In his first Excise station Burns was involved in most of the important duties. His station comprised two tanners, no fewer than eleven maltsters, two victuallers (publicans who brewed their own beer), three wine dealers, twenty-one spirit dealers, twenty-seven tobacconists, fifteen tea dealers and twenty-two compounders. Compounders were usually small victuallers who brewed infrequently and because of their distance from the officer's residence did not warrant a regular visit. They were allowed to pay a monthly sum in advance and their Excise duty was calculated and paid annually. Normally the collector decided how often the officer should survey their premises–they were known as 'cautionary visits'.

Burns would need to have a fair working knowledge of each trade. Every separate Excise duty had its own precise written instructions as to the number of visits to be made, their frequency and timing, the various control checks to be applied, what gauges and dips should be taken and the kind of accounts to be kept. Every survey, with exact details of the dips and gauges found at the time, had to be recorded in a 'specimen book', which remained on the trader's premises and was thus available to the supervisor when he made his check visits and gauges. Burns was also required to keep a daily journal, wherein he would enter all his journeys and the distances covered, the places and traders surveyed, with brief details of all the work completed at each trader. This journal had to be readily available at his residence and it was carefully inspected at regular intervals by his supervisor and collector. At the end of along and hard day's riding Burns would have to spend time in the evening entering his day's work in the various survey books, and calculate the amount of malt or beer produced according to his 'dimensions book'. This book contained the details of each maltster's and each victualler's vessels, casks and vats, which had been carefully gauged to give the quantity according to the different gauges and dips. The quantities found would then have to be converted into Excise duty and separate duty vouchers prepared for each trader, who would pay at the next siting or collection day.

There was no room for latitude in Excise work; Burns's instructions were precise and unequivocal. Furthermore, the practical checks made by his supervisor were regular and detailed and the examination of his books and accounts by not only his Collector but also by the Supervisor-General at Head Office were searching and through· and any slight slip or error demanded a written explanation. Burns would always have in his mind the general and cardinal instruction, '..you are to use your utmost diligence to prevent or detect all frauds in every branch of the revenue of the Excise under your control.'

In retrospect it might be said that Excise officers were grossly 'over-managed'; however, the system did ensure that the Excise was an honest and most efficient revenue service and was recognised as such by politicians throughout the years. The regular and frequent physical checks by the supervisors ensured that there was little or no collusion between the traders and the officers–the risk of detection was too high. One form of dishonest practice, of which the supervisors were always aware, was the 'feigned survey'. Once an officer had been technically trained and had gained some experience, he was able to know exactly the state of any brewing and malting process and could calculate not only what it should gauge today but what it should have gauged the previous day and what it should gauge on the following day and so on. Thus an officer could, at some risk of course, make certain entries in the various books in respect of the following days without having actually to visit the premises. This was called 'stamping a survey' and it was considered a heinous crime warranting instant dismissal. Indeed Thomas Paine, another famous literary Excise figure, was discharged for 'stamping a whole ride'!

Each of Burns's traders was licensed by the Excise to carry out his trade. They were obliged to declare to Burns the premises at which they intended to operate, the various processes and store-rooms and even the vessels (cisterns, vats, casks etc.) that they proposed to use in the manufacture. Each room and vessel was numbered and full details recorded on an Excise entry. The trader was also required by law to give Burns prior notice of any operation with details of the quantity of materials he intended to use. Just as the officer was bound by his strict instructions, so too was the Excise trader bound by close regulations. Indeed, it was one of the perennial complaints that Excise legislation was 'overly restrictive on trade and commerce.'–a view not particularly well-founded considering the number of brewers and distillers who prospered despite a close

Excise control for a number of centuries.

Perhaps the most complicated and time-consuming duty under his control was malt. In 1790 the Excise duty on malt in Scotland was just over 8d (3½p) a bushel and it raised some £67,000. Dumfriesshire, however, was not one of the most productive areas for barley, although it did supply grain to Glasgow, Irvine and Ayr, which were all well-known brewing areas. Nevertheless, Burns had eleven maltsters in his area and they were no doubt all farmers. He had to survey each at least five times a fortnight as well as making a certain number of visits, such as returning on the same day or early the following morning.

In simple terms malt is essentially barley that has been allowed to germinate by soaking in water and then dried by the application of heat. The time for sowing barley was from the beginning of April to the middle of May and it was then harvested from early until mid-October. The activities of the brewer and maltster were governed by the barley harvest, which of course also impinged on the Excise officer's work. The four basic stages of the malting process were steeping or wetting, couching, flooring and kiln drying. The first step was to soak the barley in a container to promote germination. In Burns's time every maltster who steeped or 'wetted' more than eight bushels of grain (quite a small quantity) at one time was required by the Excise to construct a cistern for the purpose. This was normally made of wood and lined with stone or lead; it had to be permanently fixed, the sides and ends being straight and at right angles and no deeper than 40 inches. The maltster was required to declare the total quantity of barley being used in a malting and also give prior notice to the officer of the precise time and date he intended 'to wet the grains'.

The period of soaking varied according to weather conditions and the condition of the barley and could vary from two to four days. Once the barley had been steeped, it was then drained out and laid on a floor to dry and was regularly turned until it was in the right condition to be dried in a kiln. The whole process could take up to at least two weeks and maybe more, again depending on the weather, and during the whole time Burns would be concerned with its condition. He was required to take gauges while it was in the cistern, 'on the couch', and on the floor'. As far as the Excise was concerned there was a technical difference between 'on the couch' and 'on the floor'; if barley had been out of the cistern less than thirty hours it was considered 'in couch', and if longer 'on the floor'. The various gauges taken during the process fluctuated according to the swell of grain by the absorption of water and its germination. The 'best' gauge found by Burns would be the figure used to calculate the Excise duty that was payable. The malting season lasted from November to March, so Burns would have his busy time during the worst months of the year for travel, not at all helpful to his condition of health.

Burns successfully prosecuted a farmer at Muircleugh, Thomas Johnston, for illicit malting. The decreet (a term then used in Scottish law for a judgment) was for £5, of which Burns's share would have been half, less, of course, any sitting fees. Johnston subsequently appealed against the judgment and Burns's answer to the farmer's petition has survived. Burns was obviously not pleased with the petition as it created extra work for him and furthermore he was convinced that it was an 'open and shut case'. In writing to John Mitchell, his Collector, in

September 1790 Burns touches on the two basic tenets of Excise control on any trader. Firstly he maintained that Johnston should have previously entered his premises etc. with him even though he only intended malting his barley in just one operation. Furthermore, the farmer should have given him at least forty-eight hours notice of his intention to commence malting and it was his responsibility to ensure that this notice was delivered to Burns in time. It should be noted that Muircleugh was the most northerly place in Burns's area. Unfortunately it is not known whether Johnston's appeal was successful. However, Burns's letter to Mitchell is interesting for another reason, as he ends the letter with one of his wise comments on human behaviour, which are such a feature of his prose. This time he reflects on man's mutability, '..but Time will reconcile and has reconciled many a Man to that Iniquity at first he abhorred' (C.L.p.565).

With only two victuallers in his area, the brewing of beer and ale caused him far fewer problems; although generally the brewing season in Scotland coincided with the malting season, thus making the winter months his busiest time. There were three rates of Excise duty in force at the time; strong beer at 8s (40p), small beer at 1s 4d (7p) and twopenny ale at 3s 4d (17p), each rate per barrel, in other words twelve Scottish gallons. The total duty on beer and ale in 1790 amounted to £48,100–well short of the malt figure.

Strong ale was mainly brewed by the common brewers rather than by the victuallers and was famed throughout the country for its quality and taste, with a very ready market south of the Border. The large Scottish brewers, firms like Youngers, Tennants and Aitkins, gained their reputation from and owed their prosperity to exports of Scottish strong ale. Small beer was usually brewed from inferior materials and spent grains resulting in 'a thin vapid and sour stuff', a rather uninspiring drink and usually bottled before sale. The most popular beer was twopenny or tuppenny ale, its name derived from the early days of the century when its original price was two pence a quart. It was even mentioned by name in the Act of Union and was brewed by the majority of victuallers. As Burns wrote in 'Tam O' Shanter';

Wi tippenny, we fear nae evil;
Wi usquabae, we'll face the Devil!

(C.W.p.412)

Another of Burns's verse, 'Searching auld wives' barrels..That clarty barm [dirty yeast] should stain my laurels..' refers to the Excise officer's control of brewers. There were similar strict Excise conditions applied to brewing as there were to malting. Entry of premises and details of vats and casks completed and a notice of brewing with the quantities of materials to be used in the brew had to be given to the officer at least forty-eight hours before the operation commenced. Burns would be required to visit every brewer or victualler at least three times a week and check dip the beer during the whole brewing process as well as take stock of the beer in cask at least twice a week.

The majority of farmers brewed their own beer for personal consumption and such beer was free from Excise duty; however, many brewed extra quantities for sale at markets and fairs and it was then that they were required to pay duty in advance before they had actually sold the beer. This was the only time that Excise officers actually physically collected duty. The 'bye-brewers' as they were called were so prevalent in Scotland that supervisors were instructed, '..to go to as many places where fairs, weddings etc. are kept, as you can, to see if the officers take and enter into their books true accounts of the drink sold on such occasions.'

Two of the many apocryphal stories relating to Burns's Excise life concern bye-brewers. The first tells of Jean Dunn of Kirkpatrick Durham who had brewed some beer for the local fair. She watched with some trepidation as Burns and a colleague approached her house. She left by the back door rather than answer questions on the matter, leaving her servant and her small daughter to face the officials. The servant girl, on being asked whether there had been any brewing for the fair, replied, 'O no, Sir, we hae nae licence for that.' Whereupon the little girl piped up, 'That's no true. The muckle black kist (chest) is fu o the bottles o yill that my mother sat up aa night brewin for the fair.' Burns is reputed to have replied, 'We are in a hurry just now; but as we return from the fair we'll examine the muckle black kist' Burns would expect that the chest would be empty on his return us all the beer would have been sold at the fair.

The second story emanated from a Professor Gillespie of St. Andrews, who recounts the time in 1793 when he was in Thornhill on a fair day and saw Burns call hurriedly at the door of a poor woman, named Kate Watson, who did some bye-brewing to supplement her meagre income. Burns is reputed to have said to her, 'Kate are ye mad? the supervisor and I will be in on ye in half an hour; gude bye to ye at present.' Both are nice stories and one would like to believe that Burns had sufficient compassion to bend the severity of the revenue laws in the case of poor widows doing a little trade. They may be both right but the second story seems very doubtful on the grounds that, although Thornhill was indeed situated in Burns's first Excise area, by 1793 he was stationed in Dumfries and it is highly unlikely that he would be attending a fair in Thornhill in an official capacity.

The control of the two tannaries in his area would, I imagine, be one of the more uncongenial tasks he had to perform. Each required a visit at least three times a week and extra attendance when hides and skins were being dried. As soon as he received the notice from the tanner Burns would visit the tannery to weigh every single skin and hide and carefully mark each with an Excise seal. There were precise instructions as to where each different skin should be marked, for instance horseskins on each flank and dog skins 'just above the tail'! The technical knowledge needed to understand the trade and to distinguish the various skins and hides was quite formidable. His Excise instructions contained a long glossary of terms in common use in the trade–'roundings', 'rands', 'offals', 'pates' and 'wooze' are just a few examples. The smell he encountered at the tanneries could not have been very pleasant especially as the process for 'clout' leather was described as 'after being tanned it was placed in a hole and covered with horse dung to give it a hardness and a black colour'. To add further complications there were no fewer than fourteen different rates of Excise duty depending on weight, size of skin and whether it had been dressed in oil, tanned or tawed (soaked in a solution of alum and salt). The result was that the number of accounts to be kept and the variety of vouchers to be prepared made the job particularly onerous and time-consuming.

The remainder of his Excise area, which was made up of dealers and retailers of various goods, would be relatively simple compared with the complexities of the malt, beer and leather duties. Furthermore, Burns was not restricted to a set number of visits each week but only obliged to survey as often as 'his other business would allow'. Each dealer and retailer had to keep a stock book of all the dutiable goods he received–tea, tobacco, coffee, wines and spirits–and had to produce a duty-paid permit for each new consignment. No goods could leave the premises without a permit signed by Burns. Only one such permit signed by Burns has survived, which, considering the hundreds he must have issued during his seven years in the Excise, is quite surprising. On each visit Burns would have 'to stock the premises', in other words take a physical check of the goods and compare with the trader's stock book; these books were taken up at the end of each round and a new book issued. As there were seven rounds in an Excise year Burns would have to visit every dealer and retailer every two months just to do this task. Virtually the sole purpose of this elaborate system of permits and stock books was to prevent the movement and sale of smuggled goods; that smuggling was conducted on a colossal scale and continued unabated until well into the next century shows how unsuccessful this particular Excise control proved to be.

I think it is now abundantly clear that Burns's Excise post was far from being a sinecure. The number of the hours daily that he had to devote to his Excise business were quite awesome. Considering that at the same time he was farming Ellisland, at this period of life Burns could not be accused of being idle. The more one considers the physically demanding rounds of visits and the mass of paperwork, the wonder is how Burns found the energy and the spare time to write his numerous letters, let alone any poetry as well as contribute songs to Johnson's *Musical Museum* with all the proof reading and acting as a virtual editor of the *Museum*. Certainly his days at Ellisland must have been the most hectic he had ever spent. There was never any question that allowance would have been made for the fact that he was an author as far as his Excise work was concerned. Indeed John Brown, a minor literary figure who had served in Dumfries Third Itinerary during 1792, had made several errors in his Excise work. He was reprimanded by Mitchell, the Collector, who reported, 'Mr. Brown promises every possible attention in future, now his mind is somewhat relieved as having finished his publications as an Author, which I do gladly hope will be the case.' Unfortunately it was not to be: Brown was moved to Ayr and a few years later was discharged from the Service.

How did Burns view his new profession? From his letters written in the latter months of 1789 there is no hint or suspicion that he regretted the step that he had taken. In writing to Robert Graham in December, after just four months as an officer, he admitted;

> ...I have found the Excise business go on a great deal smoother with
> me than I apprehended...Nor do I find my hurried life greatly
> inimical to my correspondence with the Muses...I meet them now
> and then as I jog through the wild hills of Nithsdale–I take the liberty
> to inclose you a few bagatelles, all of them the vagaries of my leisure
> thoughts in my Excise-rides.

(C.L.p.431)

–no complaints there about the pressure of Excise work.

Perhaps the only thing that concerned him about his new post was the effect the news would have on some of his friends. In a letter to Robert Ainslie, a friend from his Edinburgh days, Burns tried to explain why he had taken such a decision;

> ...I know how the word, Exciseman, or still more opprobrious, Gauger, will sound in your ears–I too have seen the day when my auditory nerves would have felt very delicately on this subject but a wife and children are things which have a wonderful power in blunting these kind of sensations–Fifty pounds for life, & a provision for widows and orphans, you will allow, is no bad settlement for a Poet.–For the ignominy of the Profession, I have the encouragement which I once heard a recruiting Sergeant give to a numerous if not a respectable audience on the streets of Kilmarnock–'Gentlemen for your farther & better encouragement. I can assure you that our regiment is the most blackguard corps under the crown and consequently with us an honest fellow has the surest chance of preferment'.
>
> (C.L.p.338-339)

Burns also added that he did find some 'very unpleasant and disagreeable circumstances' in the Excise business (he was not specific regarding them) but he had decided that if his present lot did not become worse, he would be quite content with life.

It was to Lady Elizabeth Cunningham, however, the sister of the Earl of Glencairn, that he best expressed his feelings on the subject. 'People may talk as they please of the ignominy of the Excise but what will support my family and keep me independent of the world is to me an important matter, and I had much rather that my Profession borrowed credit from me, than that I borrowed credit from my Profession' (C.L.p.498)–and that is precisely what has happened for the past two hundred years.

I think it is fair to say that Burns did indeed feel a certain pride in his appointment. Just as he liked to indulge himself occasionally by writing 'Robert Burns, Poet' so it is alleged that he had his snuff-box engraved 'Robert Burns, Officer of the Excise' Although the provenance of this inscription is somewhat suspect, it may have been added long after his death, I do not feel that Burns would have objected to the appellation.

BURNS' HOUSE IN DUMFRIES WHERE HE DIED, NOW A MUSEUM.

Chapter Four

The contentment that Burns had felt after a couple of months in the Excise proved to be short-lived. The sheer physical effort of combining farming with his official duties, allied to the onset of winter, had imposed too harsh a regime on his flawed constitution. At the end of November 1789 his health gave way under the strain and he suffered a debilitating attack of 'persistent headaches and weakness of limbs'. This particular bout of illness was so severe that he could barely lift his head for three weeks and he had to give up all thoughts of Excise work.

As he groaned under the miseries of a diseased nervous system, he became morbidly depressed about his situation. He was now only too aware that the farm at Ellisland had turned out to be 'a ruinous affair', which would have to be sold leaving him with the Excise as the only salvation for him and his family. Perhaps in his deep despair he also realised that his health might not survive another hard winter's riding the hills of Nith in all weathers and so he had convinced himself that the only solution was to obtain a foot-walk district in Dumfries. Early in the New Year when his condition had improved, he confessed to his brother Gilbert that 'my nerves are in a damnable state. I feel that horrid hypochondria pervading every action of both body and mind' (C.L.p.358). Yet he was back to surveying his traders though he did find himself 'in an unremitting hurry of business', possibly as a result of trying to catch up with his backlog of Excise visits.

In February his poor mare Jenny Geddes, which he had bought for £5 in Edinburgh and had carried him faithfully on his various tours, died. Like her master she had broken down under the strain of Excise hardriding and also working at the plough. A division in Dumfries, where there was no need to keep a horse, must have seemed to Burns to be a most attractive and desirable situation.

In a letter to Mrs. Dunlop, which he wrote in early March, Burns admitted that the farm was a failure and with the rent increasing by £20 a year in 1791 there seemed no other alternative but to dispose of it. The Excise, he wrote, notwithstanding all his objections to it (they were not listed), did please him tolerably well and had become his sole dependence. He did, however, confide to her that he had 'a foot-walk whenever I chuse'; so in less than two months he had achieved his ambition–a determined man as far as his future and the well-being of his family were concerned.

There is no question that Robert Graham intervened in this matter. As it is quite clear from a subsequent letter, Burns applied directly to Mitchell, his Collector at Dumfries, for a move of areas. Mitchell certainly had the authority, without recourse to Head Office, to exchange officers within his Collection as he saw fit. I have no doubt that Mitchell would have explained to Burns that normally an officer remained in an out-ride for two to three years to gain experience before he could be considered ready for a town division and Burns had only been in the Service for barely six months. However, Mitchell acceded to Burns's request, perhaps on the grounds that his application was supported by his supervisor, Findlater, who had quickly become a firm friend of Burns. What remained to be decided was the timing of the remove and who should be the hapless officer to make way for Burns.

Dear Mrs. Dunlop, who seemed to be constantly thinking of Burns's interest and well-being, enquired, almost naively, whether a certain Mr. Corbet could be of any advantage to him, because if so, she would renew an old friendship with Mrs. Corbet on his behalf. Valued and valuable friend indeed, she had picked on one of the two names in the Service that could be of great advantage to him. The 'Mr. Corbet' in question was none other than William Corbet, one of the two Supervisor-Generals at Head Office in Edinburgh. Although this rank was equivalent to that of collector, the two men had boundless power and authority over all the staff working in the collections. They were responsible for the proper collection of the duties and acted as technical advisers to the Excise Board. Both had worked their way up the slippery promotion ladder from expectant to collector and were therefore greatly experienced in the physical control of traders as well as the ultimate authorities on the books and accounts kept by the officers.

William Corbet had entered the Excise in 1773 at the age of seventeen, just before the minimum entry age was set at nineteen. Most of his early service as an officer was in Dumbarton and Glasgow and in 1784 he was appointed to a supervisor's post at Stirling. Just one year later he became a Supervisor-General in Edinburgh. To be appointed to such a senior post at the age of thirty suggests that he was an officer of rare talent with a very high reputation within the Service–his official character was shown as 'an active, good officer'. It is strange to relate however that Corbet was suspended from duty for virtually four months in 1795. The cause for this fall from grace is not known, but, it did not greatly effect his career because in 1797 he was appointed Collector at Glasgow, the most prestigious appointment outside Edinburgh. Corbet remained at Glasgow until he died in harness in 1811. By a strange coincidence his successor as Collector there was Alexander Findlater.

It is worth mentioning that apart from his connection with Burns, Corbet had another claim to fame–though slightly less praiseworthy. Corbet was a friend of the notorious Deacon William Brodie. Brodie was outwardly a quite respectable citizen, who had once been a Town Councillor in Edinburgh; but by night he led a most unsavoury life, frequenting gambling dens and associating with the criminal fraternity of Edinburgh. Brodie was convicted and hanged for his part in the robbery of the Excise Head Office. At his trial, in 1788, it was stated, 'A Mr. Corbett from Stirling had occasion to visit the Excise Office for drawing money and Brodie often accompanied him and while in the Cashier's room the idea of the robbery first came to him. He frequently made other calls at the Office under the pretence of asking for Mr. Corbett but with the sole purpose of becoming better acquainted with the premises.' The trial and the public hanging (it was said 40,000 attended) were the talking points of all Edinburgh at the time and Burns must have been fully aware of such a famous case, especially as William Creech, his publisher, was on the jury, but the *cause celebre* is not mentioned in any of his letters.

Burns's response to Mrs. Dunlop's kind offer was nothing short of enthusiastic. He said that he had set his ambition on obtaining a post as a port officer, perhaps on the Clyde at Port Glasgow or Greenock. He mentioned also that he had been considering writing to Robert Graham on the matter. Nevertheless, he freely admitted that should Corbet 'interest himself properly for him' (C.L.p.184), then Corbet could 'easily transport me to Port Glasgow, which would be the ultimatum of my present Excise hopes.'

The attendance of Excise officers at the ports originated with the 'inland' duties, as opposed to import duties collected by the Customs. The main goods liable to an extra Excise duty on import were spirits, wines, tea and tobacco. Thus at most ports, or at least the major ones, Excise port officers worked alongside Customs officers–though not in perfect harmony–measuring, weighing and gauging the very same goods. It was not until 1830 that all the Excise duties at import were passed to the Customs.

The main attraction of such a post for Burns was the increased salary (an extra £20 a year) and the strong possibility of augmenting this with fees, and, as he was quick to point out, 'as much rum and brandy as will easily supply an ordinary family'! Burns did suggest to Robert Graham, when he finally got round to writing to him on the subject, 'I have wayward feelings as appearing as a simple Gauger in a Country where I am only known by fame' (C.L.p.434). Really how serious he was in the wish is not at all clear especially as at the time (September 1790) he was already in a foot–walk district, though the idea appears to be still uppermost in his mind two years later.

As good as her word Mrs. Dunlop did renew her acquaintance with Mrs. Corbet and as a result Corbet wrote to Findlater towards the end of the year (1790), asking him to give his assessment of Burns's character and ability. It seems unlikely therefore that Burns had met Corbet previously, as some writers have suggested. Just two days before Christmas Findlater replied. He described Burns as 'an active, faithful and zealous officer, who gives the most unremitting attention to his duties ...and tho' his experience must be small as yet, he is capable, as you may well suppose, of achieving a much more arduous task than any difficulty that the theory or practice of our business can exhibit.' An excellent recommendation for any officer and one that could not have been bettered even if Burns had written it himself!

Findlater was probably Burns's most faithful Excise colleague and friend both during the poet's lifetime and afterwards when he defended Burns's name and reputation. Findlater was born in Burntisland, the son of a minister. He entered the Excise in 1774 at the age of twenty, which made him five years Burns's senior. His service as an officer was mainly in Fife, Falkirk and Glasgow. In 1786 he was promoted to examiner, which was really a trainee supervisor, and, in June 1791, he was appointed to his first post as supervisor at Dumfries. There is a certain discrepancy here, however, because Burns quite obviously knew Findlater before 1791 as his letter from Ellisland in October 1789 clearly shows. In this letter Burns describes Findlater as 'a Gentleman of which I have the highest esteem' (C.L.p.539). Also from his first days in the Excise Findlater was his supervisor and Burns maintains that the ease in which he had entered the business was largely due 'to the kind assistance and instruction of Mr. Findlater, my supervisor..' The only explanation is that John Rankine, the established supervisor at Dumfries at that time, must have been on prolonged sick leave and Findlater was sent to Dumfries to act for him–a not uncommon practice for examiners. John Rankine died in March 1791, hence Findlater's appointment in June.

The formal date of Burns's appointment to Dumfries Third foot–walk division was 25th July 1790. The officer moved to accommodate the poet was William Johnston, who was transferred into Wigtown, the neighbouring district, and was later sent to Glasgow. Burns's new Excise area covered about one third of Dumfries and he had no more than four miles to walk in total, though for the first sixteen months he had to travel the six and a half miles from Ellisland to Dumfries before he could start his work.

The new area has been called 'the Tobacco district', although it was not shown under this name in any of the Excise records. It is not too difficult to see why it gained such a title, however, because Burns had no fewer than fifty-two tobacco dealers and retailers and one manufacturer under his survey–probably a greater number than there are tobacconists in Dumfries today. As well as this great emphasis on tobacco, he had nine victuallers, a chandler and a brickmaker to visit.

On its first introduction into the country tobacco had been very lightly taxed––at 2d per lb. King James I so abhorred 'the obnoxious weed' that he tried to tax it out of existence; in 1602 the duty was 6s 8d (33p) a pound, roughly equivalent to a 1,000% duty by value! Such a massive tax quite naturally created a boom in smuggling with the result that the duty was slowly reduced. When the Excise was first introduced a small duty was placed on tobacco, but it did not survive long and for the next 140 years the only duty on tobacco was a Customs one at import. Of course during the course of the eighteenth century tobacco became one of the staple goods of the smuggler.

In an attempt to reduce the large scale smuggling of tobacco, William Pitt introduced an Act in 1789, which changed the duty charge to 6d (2½p) per lb. (Customs) and 9d (3½p) per lb. (Excise). Importers were compelled to deposit their tobacco in warehouses and when it was released for home consumption the Excise duty became payable. Elaborate arrangements were made to cover the manufacture, distribution and sale of the commodity. Dealers and retailers were required to take out licences and keep precise records. No deliveries could be made without the agreement of the Excise officer, who issued a permit for all movements of tobacco, however small. The tobacco trade universally condemned the Act and its most restrictive measures; in fact so vociferous were their complaints that a Parliamentary Commission was set up to examine the objections. The new measures were showing some success, however, the revenue from tobacco had noticeably increased and in the first year no fewer than 156 lots of seized tobacco were offered for sale in London and 34 in Edinburgh. The Act remained in force for the next forty years though whether it had a significant effect on smuggling is very doubtful. It was certainly very restrictive on all parts of the trade and was most unpopular. As the legislation had been in operation for barely one year when Burns was given the control of all the tobacco trade in Dumfries, there is no doubt that he would have suffered a fair amount of opposition and abuse at the hands of the dealers and retailers.

In addition to this new legislation Burns had two new (to him) Excise duties to learn and master–one on candles and the other on bricks. The Excise duty on candles was first introduced in 1710 with the usual Excise restrictions–licensed premises, notice of manufacture, stock books etc. In 1787, however, the chandler was compelled to provide covers and fastenings for all his utensils, which were then locked by the officer so that the poor trader could do nothing without notifying the officer. The calculation of the duty on candles was most complicated and depended on the number of cubic inches of tallow or wax found during various stages of the manufacture, which was then divided by a special factor to arrive at the dutiable quantity.

The surveying of chandlers was particularly onerous and very time consuming; they had to be visited at least twice daily and often three and four times and at the most inconvenient times. An Excise officer writing some thirty years later said of the work, 'it was the most tiresome and trying part of my work'. Before breakfast he had to go to unlock the chandler's utensils and then visit them every four hours whilst they were working. His final visit of the day was to the chandlers, to check on their day's output, weigh and take account of the candles before locking up the utensils. During the summer, he recalled, 'this was frequently as late as midnight'. This same officer has left a vivid picture of what an Excise officer looked like whilst going on his rounds. 'I was dressed in a capacious coat with large pockets to carry the malt sticks and account books and with a gauging stick in my hand (Burns called it 'a gilt-headed Wangee rod, an instrument indispensably necessary') and it the other hand a large bunch of malt-house and chandlers keys giving me the appearance of a turnkey of a prison'! He omitted to mention the ink-horn, a small vessel made of horn used for holding ink and which was normally clipped into a buttonhole. During the eighteenth century Excise officers were frequently nicknamed 'inkhorns'. It was this officer's considered opinion that his work could only be achieved by 'incessant application' and life appeared 'all work and no play with no intermissions'.

The duty on bricks was a relatively new tax and had been introduced in 1784, its express purpose to pay for the interest on the huge debt incurred as a result of the American War. As with most Excise duties the makers were licensed and the normal notice to the officers was required before any operation could commence. Once moulding and firing had started the officer was compelled to' visit daily. Looking at the instructions of the time it would appear that the Excise control of brickmakers was probably the most simple and straightforward of all the duties, with no intricate gauging, no complicated calculations and no locked utensils. It was a matter of a simple count of the bricks manufactured with a 10% allowance for 'spoiled' bricks.

There is evidence, however, that Burns already had experience of the duty on bricks because on display in the Burns Museum in Dumfries is a decreet in his handwriting against a certain 'Robert Moore in Dumfries', who was fined £1 for making bricks without an Excise entry. It is interesting to note that if Moore did not pay this fine within fourteen days he would incur an additional penalty of 2d (1p) per £1. The decreet is dated 26th October 1789, which was barely two months after Burns had entered the Excise, quite an early coup for him! It is rather mystifying to explain this offence as at the time Burns's Excise area did not extend to Dumfries nor indeed did it contain a licensed brickmaker. I am indebted to James Mackay, the Editor of the Bicentenary edition of Burns's letters, who informs me that Robert Moore was a local builder with premises in Maxweltown. He also states that brickmaking was relatively new to Scotland. It had been first introduced into the country by James Maxwell of Kirkconnel, who was the father of Dr. William Maxwell–Burns's close friend and last doctor. Maxwell had brought the technology from France when he returned from exile as a Jacobite. Krikconnel House near Dumfries, which was built by Maxwell, is the oldest brick-built house in Scotland and is constructed from local clay bricks made on the spot. During Burns's time the duty on 'common' bricks was 5s 10d (29p) per thousand and almost double for 'large' bricks. The Excise duty survived until 1850 and along with the tax on windows it was considered a penal imposition on house-building.

Burns soon appreciated that his new area contained some work unfamiliar to him, 'I am engaged in a line of our business to which I was an entire Stranger' (C.L.p.196). However, anticipating his move he had asked Peter Hill, his book-seller friend in Edinburgh, in March 1790 to supply him with *An Index to Excise Laws now in Force* by Jelinger Symons–a massive tome produced by an Excise solicitor. I doubt whether he found his new area any easier. The number of tobacco dealers would keep him busy checking and comparing their stocks and issuing permits, let alone the nine victuallers he also had under his control. So it is not surprising that he complained to Mrs. Dunlop in August about 'his long day's toil, plague and care' (C.L.p.191). Perhaps rather than face the long ride back to Ellisland after a hard day of Excise business, he slept in the upstairs bedroom of the 'Globe', his favourite Dumfries inn, where he found the convivial company, not to mention the charms of Anna Park, much to his liking. Did he use the perennial excuse, 'I was delayed in the office'?

Certainly during July 1790 Burns spent much time in Dumfries on the occasion of the election of a Member of Parliament for the town. He became quite involved in the campaign to support Patrick Miller Junior, the son of his landlord. Miller was elected and served as Member until 1796. By his actions Burns was endang-ering his Excise position. From as early as 1700 Customs officers were expressly forbidden to use any influence in elections and in 1711 this ban was extended to Excise officers. They were firmly instructed 'not to intermeddle in elections'; indeed before each election the Excise Board issued a general caution to all its staff reminding them of the embargo. From 1782 all revenue officers were excluded from even voting at elections. Although the Bill during its passage through the House of Commons was hotly contested it was nevertheless passed by a large majority. It had been calculated that revenue officers, not just the Customs and Excise but also the Post Office, Stamps and Salt officers, formed nearly twenty per cent of the total electorate and that they could 'influence 140 seats in the House of Commons'. Thus all revenue officers were debarred from any form of Parliamentary activity. Even a clause in the Reform Bill of 1832 proposing to remove the disability was rejected. It was not until 1867 that Excise officers received the vote and another eight years before they could take an active part in politics. The Excise Board took the prohibition very seriously;

some officers in England had been discharged for their political activities, though there is no evidence of any Scottish officer being dismissed on such grounds. Nevertheless Burns was sailing very close to the wind, especially in 1795 when he actively supported Patrick Heron, the Whig candidate, only a few years after the enquiry into his political views.

Burns had first visited Dumfries in 1787, on which occasion he was made a Burgess of the town, an honour he was later to put to his advantage with his sons' education. Dumfries was a historic town, having been made a Royal burgh in 1186. It was a busy commercial centre for the area, a thriving place with a population of just over 10,000 and attractively situated on the east bank of the Nith some nine miles from the Solway Firth. Many travellers had commented on its pleasing aspect and character. Smollett wrote, 'it was a very elegant trading town ... good provision and excellent wine, at very reasonable prices and the accommodation as good in all respects as in any part of South Britain. If I was confined to Scotland for life, I would choose Dumfries as my place of residence.' Not for nothing was it called 'The Queen of the South' though Burns named it 'Maggie on the Banks of Nith'.

The port, although it had its origins back in the middle ages, was not very flourishing in Burns's day. In January 1795 he commented on the distressful state of commerce of the town and its imports, 'they are no more, for one year'. One of the problems was the difficult navigation of the river, due to a shifting course at the estuary, dangerous sandbanks and the erratic tides. Some vessels arrived direct from foreign parts with timber, bark, wines and spirits. There were no direct imports of tobacco; a port had to be specially approved by the Customs Board for its import and Dumfries was not. It was in the following century that trade at Dumfries reached its peak. Most of the shipping in the late eighteenth century was coastal, to and from the Clyde and Ayrshire ports, and Burns became involved in the trade in his last Dumfries division. It is interesting to note that the Mid-Steeple, one of the main architectural features of the town, was financed in 1703 from the town's share of the sale of the tack (farm) of the Customs and Foreign Excise duties at the port.

Burns was, of course, a regular visitor to Dumfries while he was living at Ellisland. Not only did he frequent inns such as the Globe and the King's Arms, but he also regularly attended the plays presented by George Sutherland's Company at the Old Assembly Rooms. His Excise business ensured that he came to Dumfries at least eight times a year for collection day. This was the day when all Excise traders were required to attend the Excise Office to pay the duty that had accrued in the previous 'round'–some six weeks in duration. Burns would be on call should any of his charges or vouchers be queried by one of the traders and he had to produce all his books and accounts for inspection by Mitchell. On 14th July 1790, just a week or so before he took up his new division, Burns wrote from the Dumfries Excise Office, 'Coming into town this morning to attend my duty in this office, it being Collection Day' (C.L.p.260). The actual site of the office is not known but it could have been a room set aside in the Collector's residence or even an inn in the town. There was no real need for a separate building as all officers worked from their homes. It was not until the middle of the nineteenth century that special Excise offices were provided and then only in the larger towns.

The change in Excise division brought Burns into much closer contact with his fellow officers. In 1790 the most senior officer in post was Robert Erskine, who was almost sixty years of age with over half this time spent in the Service. His long experience would have been invaluable to the younger officers, and even after he retired he remained in the town. His son Robert Junior joined the Service at Dumfries but stayed for only a short time before being moved to Ayr. Another old and experienced hand was George Grey, who was well into his mid-fifties with over twenty years in the Excise. He was in Dumfries First Division and was replaced by Burns in 1792. In the Second Division was John McQuaker, a man with a large family to support, but who was not rated as a very good officer. It is quite possible that Burns already knew McQuaker, as the latter had spent four years as the officer in Mauchline. Certainly McQuaker would be aware of all Burns's unhappy relations with the Armour family.

The officer who replaced Burns in his old division was Archibald Thompson. He had arrived in Dumfries in March 1790 as a supernumerary and was only twenty-seven years old and single. Thompson was one of the several Excise officers who greatly admired Jean Lorimer–'Chloris', the attractive daughter of Burns's near neighbour, William Lorimer of Kemys Hall. Thompson was considered to be 'a slow officer that needs spurring'. It would appear, however, that nobody spurred him because he was discharged after just twelve months service! Just to confuse Burns's students there was a 'William Corbet' filling the Third Itinerary but there is no evidence to show that he was even remotely related to his illustrious namesake at Head Office. The 'Dumfries Corbet' left the town in November 1791. At Bridgend, the western suburb of Dumfries, was William Penn, only a year older than Burns but already with thirteen years of Excise experience. He had been a Collector's clerk in Ayr before arriving in Dumfries in the same year as Burns. He probably already knew Burns from his days in Ayr when Burns was being instructed and he was the only officer to remain in Dumfries throughout Burns's seven years service. Penn must have come to know Burns very well and it is a great pity that he did not leave any memory of the poet's Excise days, though he died in 1799 just before Currie's biography was published. On Burns's death Penn took over his division. There is speculation that he was the son of Matthew Penn, the Dumfries solicitor, who wrote to Burns in the last week of his life asking for payment of an overdue bill, a letter which caused the poet much worry and heartache. From Burns's letter of November 1790 to Dr. James Anderson, the editor of *The Bee* or *Literary Intelligence*–a literary and scientific periodical–we can surmise that some of his Excise colleagues were also close friends. Burns had arranged a subscription to the periodical on behalf of colleagues and friends. Findlater, Thompson and Penn were all named as was Hugh Marques and John Lewars Junior. Marques, a young man of twenty-five years, had arrived in Dumfries in September 1790 and was appointed to Woodhouse, a large country area to the east of Dumfries stretching as far as Gretna. It would be unlikely that he and Burns would meet very frequently for that reason. Marques later became a port supervisor in Leith and lived long enough to enjoy a pension for twenty years–a very rare occurrence in those days.

John Lewars Junior became Burns's closest Excise colleague during his last five years; he was reputed to be the Exciseman in 'The deil's awa ...'. He was the son of an Excise supervisor and was five years younger than Burns. In June 1790 Lewars was appointed to Dumfries Second Itinerary. John Junior was held in very high esteem by Burns; 'a young man of uncommon merits, by far the cleverest fellow I have met with in that part of the world' (C.L.p.678). Lewars was single at this time and he, too fell under the charms of Jean Lorimer. His younger sister Jessy, who lived with him, helped nurse Burns during his last illness.

The other close Excise colleague was John Gillespie, who first met Burns in September 1791 when he was posted to Dumfries as a supernumerary and moved into Woodhouse when Marques left for Glasgow. Gillespie was another suitor of 'Chloris' and perhaps as a result of his lack of success in the affair that he moved to Portpatrick, a port to the west of Dumfries where his father was a merchant. Gillespie retired early at the age of forty-three, probably due to property acquired by his wife. Indeed Burns's summed up his Excise colleagues in a letter to Robert Ainslie as, 'I have one or two good fellows here whom you would be glad to know ..' (C.L.p.340). Bound together by the unpopularity of their profession and the dangers of making friends with traders, Excisemen tended to stick together and a close camaraderie was a feature of the Excise service.

Burns had now happily settled into his life as an Excise officer, as he explained to Robert Cleghorn, a friend from Edinburgh days and the recipient of many of his bawdy verses;

...The Excise, after all has been said against it, is the business for me.–I find no difficulty in being an honest man in it; the work of itself, is easy; & it is a devilish different affair, managing money matters where I care not a damn whether the money is paid or not ..

(C.L.p.276)

The new division obviously pleased Burns as he had 'far less occupation' than in his former area and he felt confident that 'I shall be much more comfortable for my change'. This new-found confidence must have been conveyed in his letters now always in a hurry. He seems happy in his situation; a great mixture of the poet and the Exciseman: one day he sits down and writes a beautiful poem and the next seizes a cargo of tobacco from an unfortunate smuggler.' This is in direct contrast to the rather scathing views expressed by later literary writers such as Thomas Carlyle who expressed the view that 'the noblest and ablest man in all the British Isles' was merely 'gauging old tubs in the little burgh of Dumfries'. And, of course, Coleridge's famous verses, 'They snatched him from the sickle and the plough–To gauge ale-firkins'.

Unfortunately the change of air did little to improve his health–it has been suggested that the Dumfries climate was particularly bad for his condition. In October 1790 he suffered another severe bout of fever, which 'tormented' him for over three weeks and that had 'actually brought me to the grave'. There was no way during this period that he could ride to Dumfries to undertake his Excise work. At the end of January of the following year he and his horse fell–Burns was quick to point out that he had not fallen *off* his horse–however, the end result was a broken arm. He could not take up his pen for several weeks and the arm was not fully mended until April. During these periods of ill-health he must have relied on the help of his colleagues to cover his essential work otherwise his salary would have been reduced to half if a supernumerary had to be brought in and there is no evidence that this happened on these occasions.

The year 1791 started on a very high note for Burns. On 17th January he received a letter from William Corbet that informed him, 'he may soon expect to hear of his promotion'. Ten days later the Commissioners in Edinburgh formally agreed that Burns's name should be placed on the list for promotion to the rank of examiner. His name remained on this list until his death, when the word 'dead' was written in the column for date of promotion. It is now known that if he had lived until January 1797 he would have been promoted and in August of that year he would have become the Supervisor at Dunblane.

Burns had been barely sixteen months in the Excise when his name was put forward for promotion. Such a speedy rise without precedent or parallel in both the English and Scottish Excise services. The normal practice was to gain at least six or seven years experience and of that, at least, three years should be in a foot-walk division. Burns had only served for six months in Dumfries Third Division. Findlater took seven years to reach the same stage and Mitchell eight; even William Corbet required three years and that was considered very unusual. It must be accepted that Burns was an exceptional officer; it was indeed rare for any officer not to receive any reprimand in the early years of his career and certainly up to this time no errors had been found in his work. Also he had detected a very high number of offences in his first station. 'My decreet is double the amount of any Division in the District'(C. L. p. 433)–this was not idle boasting on Burns's part as such figures could be checked. Even accepting Burns's high ability as an officer, however, I think there is no doubt that the interest of Graham, Corbet and Mitchell, a most powerful and influential triumvirate, had a great effect on such early promotion. Though I hasten to add that Burns thoroughly deserved to be placed on the list, the patronage of his 'friends in high places' ensured that it was sooner rather than later.

Burns, quite rightly, was delighted with this acknowledgment of his ability and hard work. He wrote to Dr. John Moore in February;

> 'I am going on, a mighty Tax Gatherer before the Lord and have
> lately had the interest to get myself ranked on the list of Excise as a
> Supervisor. I am not employed as such, but in a few years I will fall
> into the file of Supervisorship by seniority.'

(C. L. p. 262)

The post of supervisor, he reckoned, would place him in 'a respectable situation even as an Excise-man'–he still felt the need to apologise for his profession. Oddly there is no evidence that Burns imparted the good news of his advancement to his constant supporter, Mrs. Dunlop. Although he wrote to her in February 1791 saying that it was the first time that his arm and hand had 'served in writing' there is no mention of his preferment despite the freshness of the news. It does seem an odd omission, and perhaps a letter is missing. Burns would have, no doubt, informed her when he visited Dunlop House (only about fifteen miles from Mossgiel) in June. Burns had required his Collector's approval for three days leave to attend his brother Gilbert's wedding. In those days there was no such thing as an annual leave allowance. How Burns managed to obtain a longer leave (ten days) to visit Edinburgh in December is not known, as no application to Mitchell has survived. It was on this 'Edinburgh jaunt' that Burns

NINETEENTH CENTURY PRINT OF THE SOLWAY FIRTH.

met Clarinda for the last time, which resulted in his famous love song 'Ae fond kiss' and on her side she would remember the date (December 6th) forty years later and record in her *Journal*, 'This date I can never forget. Parted with Burns in the year 1791 never more to meet in this world. Oh, may we meet in Heaven!'

As Burns said, 'life is chequered, joy and sorrow.' Just as his Excise career seemed to be progressing so well and in the pleasure of Gilbert's wedding, Burns received his first official admonishment and that it came in writing shows how serious it was. It would appear that Burns had committed two separate errors. The first was that he had recorded an incorrect quantity of stock on a brewery survey and secondly that he had not surveyed the premises as was required by his instructions. Findlater had presumably discovered the errors during one of his check surveys. Burns's reply to Findlater is worth quoting in full;

Sunday even
[June, 1791]

Dear Sir,

I am both much surprised & vexed at that accident of Lorimer's Stock. –The last survey I made prior to Mr. Lorimer's going to Edinburgh I was very particular in my inspection & the quantity was certainly in his possession as I stated it–The surveys I have made during his absence might as well have been marked *"Key absent"* as I never found any body but the lady, who I know is not mistress of keys etc. to know any thing of it, and one of the times it would have rejoiced all Hell to have seen her so drunk. –I have not surveyed there since his return. –I know the gentleman's ways are, like the Grace of God, past all comprehension; but I shall give the house a severe scrutiny tomorrow morning, & send you the naked facts. –I know, Sir, & regret deeply, that this business glances with a malign aspect on my character as an Officer; but as I am really innocent in the affair, & as the gentleman is known to be an illicit Dealer, & particularly as this is the single instance of the least shadow of carelessness or impropriety in my conduct as an Officer, I shall be peculiarly unfortunate if my character shall fall a sacrifice to the dark maneouvres of a Smuggler.

I am, Sir, your oblidged & obedient humble servant

Robt Burns

I send you some rhymes I have just finished which tickle my fancy a little

(C.L.p.540)

Until recently most editors and writers on Burns assumed that the Excise trader in question was William Lorimer, the father of 'Chloris', who was also Burns's close neighbour and friend, overlooking or being ignorant of the fact that Lorimer is a common surname in Dumfriesshire. According to *The Annals of Glencairn* , however, it was well-documented that this Lorimer was a tenant farmer at Cairnmill, half a mile southwest of Penpont. What is difficult to explain in pure Excise terms is how Burns was surveying an Excise trader near Penpont when he had left that area almost twelve months earlier. It was certainly not normal Excise practice for officers to undertake work in other areas.

It is clear from Burns's letter to Findlater that 'Lorimer' had gone on a visit to Edinburgh. This might seem to point to William Lorimer being the guilty trader. In May Burns had written a letter of introduction to an Edinburgh lawyer on behalf of Lorimer, in which he called him, 'a particular friend of mine ...a gentleman worth your knowing.' But of course it is not inconceivable that *both* Lorimer the smuggler and William Lorimer of Kemys Hall visited Edinburgh in the course of the same summer. At least thirteen families named Lorimer are known to have resided in Nithsdale in the late eighteenth century. Another Lorimer was the 'Blockhead who refused' to subscribe to the Kilmarnock Edition. If it had, indeed, been William Lorimer at fault, Burns would have transgressed one of the basic Excise principles that officers should not become friendly with their traders; indeed the 'remove system' was specifically designed to avoid this happening. If this *were* the case, and Findlater was aware of Burns's friendship with Lorimer this might have motivated him to put his complaint in writing.

Whatever the truth of the matter, and the identity of the mysterious 'Lorimer', there is no doubt that Burns was at fault in this instance. Two points need to be made. The first is that if Burns had actually made an error in the stock, rather than own up to it he shifted the blame on to Lorimer, who would have had great difficulty in challenging Burns's figure if called upon to do so. The second and more serious point is that if Burns's stock figure was correct then Lorimer had removed it without paying duty. Furthermore, if what he said in the letter was correct about Lorimer's reputation, Burns should have been far more precise and careful about Lorimer's reputation, Burns should have been far more precise and careful in his surveys. As he pointed out to Findlater, however, it was the only time that he had been at fault. On this occasion Burns was given the benefit of doubt and excused his first transgression.

In the latter months of 1791 there arrived on the Dumfries scene a man who would become Burns's closest friend during the poet's last five years. John Syme was the son of the Laird of Barncailzie–just ten miles to the west of Dumfries–and was a few years older than Burns. He had spent several years in the Army before returning to manage his father's estate. With the failure of the Ayr bank his father lost heavily and Syme was forced to find some other source of income. He managed to obtain an appointment in another revenue department as sub-distributor of Stamp duties for Dumfries. The position was not a sinecure, but as a revenue officer his life was a far cry from Burns's official life.

Stamp duties, like the Excise, had originated in the Netherlands during the early part of the seventeenth century, strangely as a result of a prize competition for a new form of tax! The original scheme required that certain legal documents should be completed on stamped paper. The duties were first introduced into this country in 1694 when a Board of Commissioners was appointed to administer the new duty and supply the necessary stamped paper.

The system of collection of the duties was unlike the Excise. The Board appointed a Distributor of Stamps. normally on a county basis, and that official appointed as few or as many sub-distributors or collectors as he felt was necessary. Syme therefore worked directly for the Distributor rather than the Board and he was most likely to be employed on a part-time basis and paid poundage at a set rate depending on the duties he collected. Wordsworth was a Distributor of Stamps in Westmorland and he had considerable problems with 'his collectors'. One went bankrupt owing over £300 in stamp duties. The remuneration was greater than the Excise salary but Syme felt a certain distaste for his job. He wrote in November 1791, 'I must mix with the noise and filth of a town and become a Tax gatherer'. In May 1793, on the death of William Maxwell, the incumbent Distributor, Syme replaced him, 'I entered into full pay, which will enable me to live better than I have been able to do hitherto.'

Though the duty was mainly imposed on legal documents, there were other stamp duties imposed at various times during the eighteenth century: on dice and playing cards, almanacks, hats, patent medicines (which survived under the control of the Excise until 1941!) and perhaps the most famous of all–the duty on newspapers. In 1849 the separate Boards of Stamps, Excise and Assessed Taxes were merged into one Board and one Department and the amalgam was named 'The Inland Revenue'. Of course, in 1909 the Excise was hived off to join with the Customs to form the present Department.

Burns and Syme first met in 1789 and they had a mutual friend in Alexander Cunningham, the Edinburgh lawyer. In August 1791 Syme dined with Burns and Findlater in Dumfries and from that date the two men became close friends. In Burns he had found a like spirit and without the poet's company he would have found Dumfries life very dull and boring, 'Were it not for his presence, I should feel a dreary blank in the society of this country.'

When Burns finally gave up his farm at Ellisland in November 1791, he moved to a house in the Wee Vennel (now Bank Street), Dumfries, where he and his family occupied three rooms and a kitchen on the second floor. On the ground floor of this house John Syme had his Stamp office, where Burns would often call, 'He [Burns] comes now and then to my office and lounges half an hour in the evening, sometimes bringing a verse or two, the skin or substance of which he bids me have no mercy on'. Syme, along with Dr. Maxwell, arranged Burns's funeral and was instrumental in urging Dr. Currie to undertake his edition of Burns's works. He also worked tirelessly to raise money for Burns's widow and children–a very true friend indeed.

Syme left some valuable reminiscences of Burns and nothing was more vivid than, 'The poet's expression varied perpetually, according to the idea that predominated in his mind: it was beautiful to mark how well the play of his lips indicated the sentiment he was about to utter. His eyes and lips, the first remarkable for fire, and the second for flexibility, formed at all times an index to his mind, and as sunshine or shade predominated, you might have told, *a priori*, whether the company was to be favoured with a scintillation of wit, or a sentiment of benevolence, or a burst of fiery indignation ...I cordially concur with what Sir Walter Scott says of the poet's eyes. In his animated moments, and particularly when his anger was aroused by instances of tergiversation, meanness, or tyranny, they were actually like coals of living fire'.

In January 1792, in a letter to Mrs. Dunlop, Burns commented on his work in his new division. He added, almost as an afterthought, '...not to mention the hunting of smugglers once or twice a week.' Thus did he sum up the most hazardous part of an Excise officer's duties. Just two weeks later the subject came up again;

> ...your unfortunate hunting of Smugglers for a little brandy; an
> article I believe indeed very scarce in your country. I have however
> hunted these Gentry to better purpose than you, and as a servant of
> my brother's goes from here to Mauchline tomorrow morning, I beg
> leave to send you by him a very small jar, sealed full of as genuine
> Nantz as ever I tasted...
>
> (C.L.p.197)

"Nantz" was the smugglers' term for French brandy and is derived from the French town of Nantes, which was an early smuggling port. There seems little doubt that this jar was part of a smuggled consignment, which had either been seized by Burns or was part of a smuggled cargo put up for auction. It could not have been obtained legally as the import of French brandy was strictly prohibited at that time. However it had come into his possession he was going against set Excise procedure. There is a popular misconception that Customs and Excise officers were allowed to retain a quantity of smuggled goods as a perquisite of their posts, but this was not so. There are instances of officers being dismissed from the two services for handling smuggled goods. Most seized goods were either sold by auction or destroyed under the supervision of a superior officer. Of course, it is perfectly feasible that Burns acquired the brandy quite legitimately at a public auction of seized goods. Robert Burns Junior, in his description of the Burns family home in Mill Street, states 'There was much rough comfort in the house, not to have been found in those of ordinary citizens; for, besides the spoils of smugglers, the poet received many presents ...'

An apocryphal Excise tale, ascribed to Ainslie, relates how Burns met a smuggler one night whilst walking by the Nith. The smuggler was not aware of who it was and offered to sell Burns some whisky. 'You've lighted on a bad merchant,' said the poet, 'I'm Robert Burns the gauger.' The man stared, but with a certain cheek, replied, 'Aye, but you're likewise Robert Burns the poet, an' I mak' sangs too; so ye'd surely ne'er ruin a brither?' 'Why friend,' said Burns, 'the poet in me has been sacrificed to the exciseman; so I should like to know what superior right you have to exemption.' A good story, with a sharp reply that has all the hallmarks of Burns.

More serious, however, is the imputation that Burns might on occasion supply smuggled goods to his friends. That is the assumption conveyed by a letter of April 1793, written to Maria Riddell, in which he said that he had managed to obtain French gloves for her. Mrs. Maria Riddell was the captivating young lady who replaced Clarinda in his platonic affections. As Burns pointed out to her;

> ...FRENCH GLOVES are contraband goods, & expressly
> prohibited by the laws of this wise-governed realm of ours.–A
> Satirist would say, that this is one reason why the ladies are so fond
> of them; but I, who have not one grain of GALL in my composition,
> shall alledge, that it is the PATRIOTISM of the dear Goddesses of
> man's idiolatry, that makes them so fond of dress from the LAND
> OF LIBERTY & EQUALITY...
>
> (C.L.p.602)

It was during a sweep search of Dumfries by Burns and his colleagues that he claimed to have;

> ...discovered one Haberdasher, who, at my particular request, will clothe your fair hands as they ought to be, to keep them from being profaned by the rude gaze of the gloting eye, or–Horrid!–from perhaps A RAPE by the unhallowed lips, of the Satyr Man.–You will remember though, that you are to tell no body, but the ladies of your acquaintance, & that only on the same condition so that the secret may be sure to be kept, & the poor Haberdasher not ruined by his kindness...

(C.L.p.603

Is this an example of Burns quite lightly jeopardizing his Excise position? If his letter is read quite literally then this must seem to be the case. It would have been in keeping with his character to wish to impress this young lady with his ability to supply her with something her superior position and money could not provide, especially as it was at the early stage of their relationship. Moreover, what is fact is that Excise 'sweeps' on retailers to search for prohibited goods were certainly used as accepted Excise controls, and indeed there were many successful Excise prosecutions made by these methods. It is much more likely, however, that Burns was merely writing in a most romantic style, and that the letter was a most extravagant and flattering piece of correspondence without any basis of fact.

Certainly the south-west coast of Scotland from Southerness Point to the Cumbraes was a notorious smuggling area. With the numerous creeks, inlets and bays the Solway coast was ideal for the illegal trade. Large cutters, wherries and luggers made the short sea passage from the Isle of Man, Northern Ireland and Port rush, a smuggling entrepôt just north of Dublin, bringing tea, brandy, tobacco and a variety of French goods. Against these smuggling ships were pitted the small force of revenue vessels. The Scottish Excise operated the *Royal Charlotte* and the *Royal George,* both large vessels of over 200 tons, well manned and heavily armed. Highland Mary Campbell's father had served on the *Royal George,* but had to retire early because of the loss of an eye in one of the bloody affrays. The Scottish Customs had five smaller vessels in service, three operating from the Clyde.

Outright sea battles were not uncommon around the coasts and in October 1783 a 16-gun Customs cutter engaged a larger smuggling vessel called the *Thunderer,* which was well loaded with tea and spirits. The *Thunderer* carried 24 guns and had a crew numbering over 70. The fight was short and brutal. The Customs vessel suffered extensive damage to its rigging and several shots below the waterline, which made it necessary to withdraw from the action. The *Thunderer* was thus free to land its cargo at its leisure and unopposed.

The scourge of the revenue forces in the area for many years was Jack Yawkins and his cutter *Hawke,* which gained an almost invincible reputation. In 1787, however, he and his vessel were finally captured by an Admiralty cruiser. Despite the *Hawke's* renown it was not considered to be 'a good enough sailor' to be used in the Revenue service and was accordingly broken up. Yawkins was used by Sir Walter Scott as the model for Dirk Hatteraick in *Guy Mannering.* Even today there is a spot on the Solway coast which is called Hatteraick's Cave.

Considering the amount of smuggling that was taking place along the Solway during Burns's time, it is quite surprising that there is only one recorded smuggling incident in which we know for certain that he was involved. This is, of course, the famous seizure of the smuggling vessel *Rosamond,* which has caused so much debate and speculation.

The Edinburgh *Evening Courant* of Thursday, 8th March 1792 reports the incident in fairly restrained terms. It stated that on the previous Wednesday [29th February] 'the revenue officer for Dumfries, assisted by a strong party of the 3rd regiment of dragoons, seized a fine large smuggling vessel at Sark-foot [a small village in the parish of Gretna at the mouth of the river Sark]...Upon the officers and the military proceeding towards the vessel, which they did in a martial and determined manner, over a broad space of deep water, the smugglers had the audacity to fire upon them from their swivel guns, loaded with grape shot; but the vessel (owing to its construction) lay in such a situation as prevented their having a direction with effect. At last, however, seeing the determined measures that they were adopting, they all deserted the vessel. Mr. Manly, the quartermaster [of the Dragoons] who commanded, behaved with much resolution and propriety, and the whole party followed his example.'

Fortunately the journal of Walter Crawfurd, the Excise riding officer for Dumfries collection, has survived for the months of January and February 1792. From this record the precise details of the incident and Burns's part in it can be established.

Crawfurd was appointed to his post in January 1792, having come from Edinburgh where he had served in the South Fencibles. His sole duty was to patrol the coast from Dumfries to Gretna in order to gain information on smuggling activities and to prevent the landing of smuggled goods. He made his residence at Annan and quite obviously worked closely with the Excise officers as well as the military.

The early entries for January show clearly how boring, frustrating and difficult his job was. Most evenings and nights he was out on patrol 'surveying the coast' and 'learning more of the routes'. For one whole day in the middle of the month he was out with William Craig, the Annan officer, 'to learn more of the country'. By 21st January he had struck lucky and had gained information of a proposed smuggling run by a lugger called *Spinder*. He rode into Dumfries to inform Findlater of the news. Although he was out regularly during the following week he found nothing to report. Finally, he heard that the vessel had been taken at sea by a Customs cutter.

For two whole days in February he rode out with Findlater and the following day he was with John Gillespie, the officer at Woodhouse, their intention being 'to learn the residences of the Smugglers and the roads frequented by them.' Some days later he teamed up with a party of dragoons, but more often than not he rode alone and most of his nights ended with the same report—'saw nothing'. One night he spent watching 'about Hopses, the residence of Mr. McDowall, the principal smuggler in this Part.'

On 26th February (Sunday) he had stayed up all night watching at Brewhouses, a known landing spot. During the night he must have received some information about a future run, because by the afternoon he had arrived in Dumfries to inform the Supervisor and the other officers that a smuggling run was expected that week. Crawfurd had left a reliable person at the spot, 'to ride Express to me on the first appearance of a Landing.'

At eleven o'clock on the evening of 27th his 'Express' arrived in Dumfries with the news that a landing was about to be made. Crawfurd, along with John Lewars, set off immediately, leaving Burns, Penn and Rankine to follow as quickly as possible. Crawfurd and Lewars arrived at Annan by the early morning and with a small party of dragoons they searched McDowall's and other smugglers' houses before arriving at the shore by midday of 28th. To ensure complete accuracy of Burns's part in the affair, the journal is quoted in full including all the mis-spellings!

> ...where I was informed that the Vessel could not get off for want of watter. I made an attempt to Board her with the Millitary but when wee offered to appoch her they hailed us that they would fire on us if wee appoched any farther.
>
> As my party had only Pistols and were but few in number and a great number of men appearing to be on Deck I stoped the Soldiery and riding up to the Vessel allone asked liberty to Come on board which after some altercation they granted. I Boarded her and found Twenty four men under arms with fifteen round of shott each. I returned to shore and consulting with the Officers and Millitary wee agreed that greater force would be absolutely necessary. In consequence of which Mr. Lewars sett off for Dumfries to Bring Twenty four more Dragoons while I went to Ecclefechan for the Party there with which I patroled the roads till the arrivall of Mr. Lewars with the additionall force from Dumfries.
>
> On the 29 m 9 wee approched the Vessall with the following force Dragoons from Dumfries Twenty Three, Annan Thirteen, Ecclefechan Eight, in all Forty four fully accoutered and on horse-back. The vessal having fallen down the Sollway Firth abouth a mill [*sic*] from where she was yesterday and being about a mile within sea mark, most of which space being covered with watter, and a very heavy Currant between us and the Vessall we deemed it impossible to get at her either on fott or on horseback, so we aggread to search the coast for Boats in which to board her. But the Country People guessing our design got the start on us and staved every Boat on the Coast before we Could reach them, the vessel in the mean time keeping up a fire of grape shott and musquetry, we resolved at last resource to attempt the passage on fott as the quick sands made the ridding on horseback dangerous or rather impossible.
>
> Wee drew up the Millitary in three divisions determined to approch her & attract her if the sream was fordable, one party fore and aft and the third on her Broadside, The first party being Commanded by Quarter Master Manly, the Second by my self and the Third led by Mr. Burns.
>
> Our orders to the Millitary were to reserve there fire till within eight yards of the vessel, then to pour a volley and board her with

sword and Pistol. The vessel keept on firing thou without any
damage to us, as from the situation of the ship they could not bring
their great guns to bear on us, we in the mean time wading breast
high, and in Justice to the party under my Command I must say with
great alacrity; by the time we were within one hundred yards of the
vessel the Crew gave up the cause, gott over side towards England
which shore was for a long long way dry sand. As i still supposed
that there were only Country people they were putting ashore and
that the Crew were keeping under Cover to make a more vigourous
immediate resistance, we marched up as first concerted, but found
the vessel compleatly evacuuated both of the Crew and every
movable on board except as per inventory, the Smugglers as their
last instance of vengene having poured a six-pounder Carronade
through her Broadside. She proved to be the Roseomond of
Plymouth, Alexander Patty Master and about one hundred tons
burthen, schooner ...

The second document attached to the journal was a list largely in Burns's
writing of the expenses incurred in watching and repairing the vessel ready for
sale. It cost £17 10s to maintain the fishermen, carpenters, dragoons and 'one &
often two Excise offrs. aboard'. It is very likely that Burns spent some time on
board. The vessel and its furniture was put up for sale by 'publick roup' in the
Coffee House, Dumfries on 19th April and made by sale £166 16s 6d. The total
expense for re-fitting etc was £45 15s 4d, thus giving the net proceeds as £121 1s
2d. From this sum the Crown would take half, leaving the reminder to be shared
out by nearly fifty persons. It is unlikely that Burns received more than £2 for
waiting almost a day and a half on a cold and wet marsh as well as risking his life.
The four-pounder carronade guns mounted on carriages with tackle were reputed
to have been bought by Burns for £3.

Burns's share in the incident was first described in Lockhart's *Life of Robert
Burns* published in 1828. Lockhart paints a most highly coloured version of the
story. According to him Burns put himself at the head of the dragoons and waded,
sword in hand, to the vessel and was the first to board her, whereupon 'the crew
lost heart, and submitted, though their numbers were greater than those of the
assailing force'. Lockhart also maintained that not only did Burns buy the four
carronades but that he sent the guns with a letter to the French Convention,
requesting that body to accept them as a mark of his admiration and respect.
However, the guns plus the letter were stopped by the Customs at Dover.

Lockhart gave as his authority 'the private journal of one of the excisemen
now in my hands'. It was later disclosed, however, that he had received certain
documents from Joseph Train, the Supervisor of Excise at Castle Douglas, who
was a very enthusiastic antiquary and had been in the habit of supplying Sir Walter
Scott, Lockhart's father-in-law, with certain suggestions and stories for the
Waverley novels. Train supplied Lockhart with Crawfurd's Journal and the two
documents, as well as allegedly a document written by John Lewars 'detailing the
circumstances of Burns having purchased the four carronades at the sale.' Train
said that he had acquired these documents from Lewars's widow and that 'Mrs.
Burns, before her death, publicly admitted the truth of these statements.'

Several biographers of Burns have doubted the veracity of 'the carronade story' and even one (Snyder) suggested that the *Rosamond* affair 'should be deleted from any life of Burns'!

In 1934, however, when the Abbotsford Papers were transferred to the National Library of Scotland, Crawfurd' journal and two attached documents were discovered but NOT Lewars's statement. It is extremely unfortunate that the only written evidence to support this story should be missing. Furthermore, there is no evidence in any extant Customs and Excise records of the four carronades being seized at Dover. The whole story becomes even more suspect when it is reputed that in 1825 Sir Walter Scott investigated the affair and applied to the Customs, who after, considerable search, found that the carronades had been seized at Dover. There is no evidence whatever in the Customs records of Scott's enquiry. This does, indeed, seem strange, as it was common practice in all ports for each letter received by the Collector, whether it came from the Board or an individual, to be copied into a bound 'letter book' with a copy of the reply. There is no evidence of any correspondenced with Sir Walter Scott in the Dover records and I find it difficult to believe that an enquiry from such distinguished and well-known person as Sir Walter would not have been recorded in the letter books. When one considers how Lockhart 'interpreted' Burns's part in the *Rosamond* affair from Crawfurd's journal, the whole sorry tale of the carronades seems most suspect. On the evidence, or rather the lack of evidence, one must consider Burns not guilty on this charge.

Another reason to throw doubt on Lockhart's veracity is his statement that Burns had composed 'The Deil's awa wi' th' Exciseman' impatiently waiting for Lewars to return with the dragoons on that fateful day. Now this highly romantic notion has been shown to be utterly incorrect by a letter from Burns that came to light in 1902–though indeed the full text was previously known. The letter dated April 1792 was addressed to John Leven, who had been appointed the second General Supervisor in 1791;

> ...Mr. Mitchell mentioned to you a ballad which I composed & sung at one of his Excise-court dinners: here it is.–
>
> The deil's awa wi' th' Exciseman–Tune, madam Cassey
> (C.W.p.467)
>
> If you honor my ballad by making it one of your charming, bon vivant effusions, it will secure it undoubted celebrity...

(C.L.p.614)

In point of fact, all that Burns was saying here is that he sang the song at an Excise dinner. He did not imply that it was rendered extempore on that occasion. Indeed, from other eye-witness accounts, it is traditionally believed that the song was composed in a house in Annan (now the Café Royal) where Burns habitually lodged. An engraved tablet commemorates the composition there.

Tantalisingly, there is no mention in the letter of the *Rosamond* incident. In fact Burns never remarked in any of his letters about the affair. Perhaps he felt that in the end it was a lot of fuss about nothing and much time had been wasted in very trying and uncomfortable conditions for very little recompense. Certainly wading through the cold Solway water could not have improved his complaint.

Chapter Five

Most writers have given February 1792 as the date of Burns's third and final change of Excise division. However, it is quite clear from the Excise records that Burns was formally appointed to his new area–Dumfries First Foot-walk–on 26th April 1792 though he did not move until 5th May. Furthermore most have suggested that it was a promotion but it was nothing of the sort. Burns was still an officer, and it was purely a matter of an exchange of divisions with the elderly George Grey. Part of the confusion has been caused by Burns's letter to Maria Riddell in February of that year wherein he informs her;

> ...I have just got an appointment to the first or Port Division as it is
> called, which adds twenty pounds per annum more to my salary. My
> Excise Income is now Cash paid, Seventy pounds a year: and this I
> hold untill I am appointed Supervisor. So much for my usual good
> luck. My Perquisites I hope to make worth 15 to 20£ more...
>
> (C.L.p.601)

There seems to be no doubt that the exchange was engineered by William Corbet, Supervisor-General. The only two surviving letters to Corbet relate directly to this move. In February Burns wrote about 'the practicality of getting into a Port Division' as he knew that 'General Supervisors' were 'omnipotent in these matters'. In this fact he was obviously quite correct because within two months Burns had received the Excise Board's approval for the exchange–I must assume that Robert Graham had also played a part. In September Burns wrote a letter of thanks to Corbet although he suggested that 'a simple letter of thanks will be a very poor return for so much kindness..' (C.L.p.598). His letter acknowledged his debt to the two ladies–Mrs. Corbet and Mrs. Dunlop.

Without doubt Burns's new division was the most difficult and complex area in the Dumfries district. He was now responsible for the only common brewery in the town; this was owned by Gabriel Richardson, his friend, who became Provost of Dumfries in 1801. Besides the brewery Burns controlled 9 victuallers, 6 tanners, 3 tawers (white leather), 2 chandlers, 1 maltster and over 50 dealers in Excise goods (wines, spirits and tea). The extra £20 salary covered his attendance at the port where he was responsible for all imported and exported Excise goods. He was also issued with the only cambric stamps in the district; the Excise duties on cambrics were most complicated and called for a sound knowledge in home and foreign textiles manufacture.

The amount of Excise duties collected by Burns were the highest in the district and the second highest in the collection. A large percentage of these duties was accounted for by wines and spirits. For this very reason Burns had been issued with the only official hydrometer in the district. Indeed in August 1792 he was at Annan Waterfoot–'this wild place of the world'–supervising the discharge of a vessel of rum from Antigua, which would have meant that he would be taking samples of rum to test the strength of the spirit for duty payment.

The testing of spirits by use of a hydrometer dated from the early part of the eighteenth century. The earliest official reference to one is in 1762 when an instrument devised by Samuel Clarke had come into general use in the Excise. Prior to this instrument an areometer had been used to work out the specific gravity of liquors, on the theory that the heavier the gravity the stronger was the spirit and vice versa–a rather cumbersome and very inaccurate method. Although Clarke's instrument was a great improvement, it was not easy to use with over forty different weights to be used depending on the temperature. By 1787 the Excise Board had acknowledged that this hydrometer was inaccurate and the search was on for an improved and more dependable instrument. However, it was not until 1816 that the famous Sikes's hydrometer was accepted by the Excise (it was in continual use until 1980). So Burns would have been issued with a Clarke's hydrometer. Indeed in 1930 a hydrometer and thermometer reputed to have been used by him was offered for auction. The provenance of the instrument was based upon its possession by the Murray family–David Murray had been Deputy Controller of Excise for Scotland in Burns's time. Whether this hydrometer was actually used by Burns is not known for certain as the design of the instrument barely changed during the time it was in use in the Excise. The maker's serial number is shown as '14162' whereas in the Excise records Burns's instrument is shown as '31' but perhaps this was merely an Excise number.

Burns himself confirmed that he found his new division quite difficult. In his letter to Corbet in September he pointed out;

> ...my new division holds me so busy and several things in it being
> rather new to me, my time has hitherto been totally engrossed.
>
> (C.L.p.599)

Fortunately one Excise record has survived that tells quite clearly just how well Burns coped with his new work. Alexander Findlater's Supervisor's diary for '8th Round, 85th Year'–that is from 10th June to 21st July 1792–has surfaced again in the last thirty years. The sixteen page diary shows the routine surveys and checks that Findlater made on all the officers in his district during the six weeks in question.

It is interesting to note in the very first entry in the diary–Monday 11th June 1792–that Findlater spent the whole day with Robert Burns. The Excise method of recording time was used throughout the diary. Findlater shows that he arrived at 'Mp7' and left at 'Ep5'–in other words at any time between the hours of 7 o'clock and 8 in the morning and between 5 and 6 o'clock in the evening. This method of recording time was a survival of the medieval system before the advent of minute hands on clocks and when they chimed only on the hour. This system of recording times was used in the Excise until about ten years ago.

During the course of the day Burns and Findlater visited the brewery, eight victuallers, eight wine and spirit dealers, two tanneries, two tawers, three chandlers and a tea dealer–a very full day's work. Findlater not only checked gauged quantities of beer but he weighed and tested stocks held by the various Excise traders; he also went back over the entries Burns had made in the different stock accounts and survey books since his last visit. Clearly Burns was under a close and rigorous supervision and Findlater could not help but know whether or not Burns was applying himself as he should.

In point of fact Findlater did during the whole day's examination find one or two slips in Burns's work, jut minor errors or 'some trivial Inadvertancies'. There was a small discrepancy in one of the stocks of dutiable tea. The Supervisor had to ask himself, if it was a reduction in stock, where had the tea gone? If it was an increase, how had the dealer obtained the tea? Had it been smuggled? He would have expected the officer to have posed similar questions, otherwise the check of stocks was pointless. In Burns's case the difference was 144 lbs and with the Excise duty it was not a small amount of money involved. However, Findlater found it was due to a mere clerical error of crediting 160 lbs instead of 16 lbs and he was pleased to see that Burns had noticed the error and put it right on his next visit to the trader. Findlater just remarked 'rectified the succeeding survey'.

At one of the victuallers, however, Burns had previously authorised the delivery of ten gallons of foreign brandy and had issued the necessary permit but had not shown the consequential reduction in the dutiable stock on hand. In this instance Burns was ordered to be admonished by the Supervisor-General. The formal rebuke was not for the initial error but for Burns's laxity in not righting the error on his next two visits to the trader, as Findlater remarked 'Nor the two succeeding surveys'. The diary shows clearly in the margin that Burns should be admonished and so he was, although Mitchell, his Collector, made no comment. The formal rebuke was a model of brevity, 'Examined J.M. Admonish J.F. Done J.C.' In all truth the errors were of a very trivial nature but such was the high standard demanded of Excise officers, and in the main attained, that such small discrepancies rated an official caution. Burns was in good company; three other officers were similarly warned.

There is an interesting observation made on a visit to another victualler. On the very day that Burns took over the new area (8th May) he had visited at some time after eight in the evening to check gauge some stock for duty purposes. This same stock had already been gauged by George Grey, the previous officer, earlier the same day. Burns's gauge found 17 gallons more than Grey's–there seems to be the makings of a good story here. Perhaps Burns was aware of the doubtful reputation of the victualler and had decided to slip in late in the day to catch him off his guard. Indeed, the trader was probably quite unaware that Burns had taken over from Grey and thus had no time to conceal the stock. Findlater accepted Burns's gauge and put the discrepancy down to 'the fraudulency of the trader'.

Findlater ended his report on his full day with Burns with the general comments on his performance, 'Mr. Burns had but lately taken charge of this Division and from that cause, and his inexperience in the Brewery branch of business, has fallen into these errors but promises, and I believe will bestow, due attention in future, which indeed he is rarely deficient in.' This last comment was as near as any Excise officer could expect to come to a very handsome compliment.

After such a long and intensive examination of Burns's work Findlater did not make another check visit until the following Monday 18th June. On this occasion he merely accompanied Burns at 6 o'clock in the evening to a tannery and two tawers to take an account for duty. Then two weeks later he again spent practically a whole day with Burns. They visited the brewery, a number of tanneries and various spirit and wine dealers, and made a thorough examination of all Burns's books and accounts. His comments on this day's work were, 'observed nothing materially amiss'. Another supervisory visit on 9th July, again to some tanneries, called forth no remarks whatsoever.

Such close supervision–four separate control checks spread over six weeks—was not unusual. All Excise officers were subjected to the same strict inspection of both their practical and written work. The high standard of efficiency and honest achieved by the Excise Service, which was unique in the revenue services of the eighteenth century, owes much to this system of management. It must also be remembered that these supervisory checks were repeated each round, so Findlater checked Burns's work on average at least thirty times a year. Thus he was the closest and most knowledgeable official to comment on Burns's perform-ance as an Excise officer and, as such, his opinion must be of great value. In defence of Burns's reputation after his death, Findlater wrote in 1818, 'he was exemplary in his attention as an Excise officer, and was even jealous of the lease imputation on his vigilance'. Fine and very well-deserved praise from an officer who reached the heights of the Scottish Excise.

By September 1792 Burns must have been very pleased with what he had managed to achieve during the previous nine months. His part in the *Rosamond* affair had been well noted at Head Office. He had obtained the desired Port Division and was coping well with the new work. His promotion to examiner seemed secure–all this and a valuable and welcome addition to his salary. He still felt the need, however, to apologise for his profession. Thus he wrote to Alexander Cunningham in September,

> 'Amid all the hurry of business, grinding the faces of the Publican and the Sinner on the merciless wheels of the Excise.'

(C.L.p.465)

Then during the next three months he was to endanger not only his promotion prospects but his very Excise post by some unwise and rather naive actions.

The last decades of the eighteenth century were times of political ferment and revolt and it would have been impossible for a man of Burns's temperament and sympathies to let the American War of Independence and the French Revolution pass unremarked. As Tom Paine said, 'These are times that try men's souls.' In 1792 with the Reign of Terror raging in France and the Society of Friends of the People urging reforms in Britain, the Government felt that the country was on the verge of revolt. By midsummer anyone who merely expressed sympathy with the French was branded a traitor. By the end of the year any person expressing even mild criticism of the Government was deemed to be a Jacobin.

At the centre of this maelstrom was Thomas Paine, the spokesman for English radical views. Paine had entered the Excise in 1762 and was discharged three years later 'for stamping his whole ride'–declaring that he had visited his traders when he had not been near their premises. Twelve months later he petitioned the Excise Board to be re-engaged and in 1768 he was appointed to a post at Lewes in Sussex. In 1772 he published a pamphlet on the inadequacies of

Excise officers' pay, a well-argued and cogent work, which did little to endear him to the Board–nevertheless he remained in post. Two years later, however, he left his Excise station of his own volition and was discharged 'in absentia'. His pamphlet *Common Sense,* written in America in 1776, crystallized the arguments for the Colonies' independence and had an important bearing on the outbreak of the War. His *Rights of Man,* written in two parts and published in 1791 and 1792, was a defence of the French Revolution and a well-reasoned demand for reform and changes in the British Constitution. The *Rights of Man* was deemed to be a seditious publication and banned, though it is estimated that over a quarter of a million copies were sold. Paine was tried and convicted for sedition in December 1792 though it was in his absence as he had escaped to France. The Government's anger and frustration were vented on the printers and distributors of the work; some were imprisoned and a few transported. Effigies of Paine were burned throughout the country and the very mention of *The Rights of Man* brought forward instant cries of 'traitor.'

In such a volatile climate Burns should have realised, if not by his past experiences, then at least from the fact that he was a Government servant, that he was not free to make political statements or fine gestures. It showed a certain naiveté on his part to believe that he could show any admiration or affection for the Jacobin cause.

The Theatre Royal, Dumfries, which had first opened in September 1792, held a special gala performance on 30th October for the Caledonian and the Dumfries & Galloway Hunt. There was a very distinguished audience that night including, of course, Burns. When 'God Save the King' was called for at the end of the play, there were vociferous and counter cries for 'ca Ira', the song of the French Revolutionaries. This outcry was drowned by the singing of the National Anthem, during which Burns allegedly kept his hat on and remained firmly seated–an obvious sign of defiance at a time when public feeling was running so high against the French.

In the following month Burns wrote a prologue for the benefit night of one of the leading actresses. It was rather provocatively called *'The Rights of Women'*, echoing Paine's publication. It even had one line, 'And even children lisp the Rights of Man'. It was almost as if Burns was deliberately tempting providence, especially as in the same month he wrote to Captain William Johnstone, a well-known Edinburgh radical. Johnstone was founder and editor of the *Edinburgh Gazetteer,* which advocated Parliamentary reform and was strongly critical of the Government. In the light of this it was rather foolhardy of Burns to send Johnstone a copy of 'The Rights of Women' for publication. However innocuous the piece was, the mere fact that he wished to contribute to such a radical journal, let alone subscribe to it as was the intention of his letter, made him suspect in the eyes of the Excise Board.

These were the outward or public demonstrations of his views, but he probably expressed stronger feelings while holding court at either the 'Globe' or the 'King's Arms' and it is unlikely that such comments would pass unremarked. As he explained to Mrs. Dunlop on 6th December, 'this part of the Country have many alarms of the Reform or rather the Republican spirit'. He went on to describe the 'ca Ira' incident at the theatre, so it had obviously made some

BURNS' MONUMENT AT DUMFRIES.

impression on him. He then states;

> ...For me, I am a *Placeman,* you know; a very humble one indeed,
> Heaven knows, but still so much as to gag me from joining in the
> cry. What my private sentiments are, you will find out without an
> interpreter...
>
> (C.L.p.202)

Less than three weeks later Burns was informed by Mitchell, his Collector, that he had received an order from the Excise Board to enquire into Burns's political conduct and to examine the charge that he was 'a person disaffected to the Government'. This news appeared to come as a bombshell to Burns though in all honesty it should not have, as he must have been aware that he was treading on thin ice. Perhaps Mitchell had intimated to him just serious the charges were. Burns immediately turned to his friend on the Board–Robert Graham.

His letter to Graham was dated 31st December and shows Burns in a most hysterical and obsequious light;

> ...Sir, you are a Husband–& a father–you know what you would
> feel, to see the much-loved wife of your bosom, & your helpless,
> prattling little ones, turned adrift into the world, degraded &
> disgraced from a situation in which they had been respectable &
> respected & left almost without the necessary support of a
> miserable existence–Alas, Sir! must I think that such, soon, will be
> my lot! And from the damned, dark insinuations of hellish,
> groundless Envy too!–I believe, Sir, I may aver it, & in the sight of
> Omnipotence, that I would not tell a deliberate Falsehood, no, not
> though even worse horrors, if worse can be, than those I have
> mentioned, hung over my head; & I say, that the allegation,
> whatever villain has made it, is a LIE! To the British Constitution,
> on Revolution principles, next after my God, I am most devoutly
> attached!–You Sir, have been much & generously my
> Friend–Heaven knows how warmly I have felt the obligation, how
> gratefully I have thanked you–Fortune, Sir, has made you powerful
> & me impotent; has given you patronage & me dependence–I would
> not for my *single Self* call on your Humanity; were such my insular,
> unconnected situation, I would despise the tear that now swells in
> my eye–I could brave Misfortune, I could face Ruin: for at the
> worst, 'Death's thousand doors stand open;' but, Good God! the
> tender concerns that I have mentioned, the claims & ties that I, at
> this moment, see & feel around me, how they ennerve Courage &
> wither Resolution! To your patronage, as a man of some genius, you
> have allowed me a claim; & your esteem, as an honest Man, I know
> is my due: to these, Sir, permit me to appeal; & by these may I
> adjure you to save me from that misery which threatens to
> overwhelm me, & which, with my latest breath I will say it, I have
> not deserved...
>
> (C.L.p.435)

Graham replied by return of post and kindly outlined the evidence that had supported the call for an Inquiry into Burns's conduct. Burns in a long letter dated 5th January answered each charge in detail.

He scoffed at the notion that he was 'the head of a disaffected party in Dumfries'. In fact he averred that no such party–either republican or reform existed in the town, unless it consisted of 'such obscure, nameless beings as precludes any possibilities of my being known to them or they to me'. As to the 'ca Ira' incident, he admitted to being at the theatre on the night and that one or two of his friends joined in the outcry but he strongly maintained that he knew nothing about 'the plot or ever opened my lips to hiss or huzza, that, or any other Political tune whatever'. Burns re-affirmed his loyalty to the King and asserted that he had 'never uttered any invectives against the king'; he had obviously conveniently forgotten the verse scratched on the Stirling window, which had caused such trouble just before he was accepted into the Excise. On this charge he cleverly hinted at his freemasonry connections perhaps he felt this would give him some extra protection in high places.

Burns's explanation of the *Gazetteer* charge was that he was merely acting for some friends, who thought that the publication was 'manly and independent'. The implication was that he was an agent in the matter. If only the Excise Board had seen the letter to Johnstone wherein Burns exhorted him;

> ...Go on, Sir! Lay bare, with undaunted heart and sturdy hand, that
> horrid mass of corruption called Politics and State-craft.
> (C.L.p.681)

they might not have accepted Burns's claim to innocence. He was quite prepared to stop the subscription if Graham thought that he had acted improperly. As to 'The Rights of Women' Burns maintained that it had nothing to do with politics!

On the more general charges of reform and his attitude to France, he maintained that he thought that the British Constitution, as settled at the Revolution [1688], was 'the most glorious on earth...but that we have a good deal deviated from the original principles of that Constitution; particularly, that an alarming System of Corruption has pervaded the connection between the Executive Power and the House of Commons–This is the Truth, the whole truth, of my Reform opinions'. He owned up to being 'an enthusiastic votary' of France in the beginning but now that the country was seeking conquests, he had altered his sentiments.

Now the strange thing is that on the very same day that he gave his replies to the charges in the letter to Graham, he also wrote to Mrs. Dunlop;

> ...the political blast that threatened my welfare is overblown.–I
> have corresponded with Commissioner Graham, for the Board had
> made me the subject of their animadversions; & now I have the
> pleasure of informing that all is set to rights in that quarter...
> (C.L.p.204)

Did Burns assume that his letter to Graham was sufficient to clear his name, or had he been informed by Mitchell that *he* was happy with his enquiries?

The situation becomes clearer from Burns's letter of April 1793 to John Erskine of Mar. Although the two men had never met, Erskine had heard a rumour that Burns had been dismissed from the Excise for his radical and republican views and he offered to head a subscription on the poet's behalf. Burns in thanking Erskine explained what had happened. It would seem that Graham laid Burns's explanatory letter before the Board and some of the Commissioners took grave offence at Burns's comments about corruption. As a result William Corbet was sent to Dumfries to enquire into Burns's conduct. This must have been a week or so after Burns's letter to Mrs. Dunlop when he considered himself cleared. Corbet, it would appear, gave Burns a very strong warning;

> ...that *my* business was to act, not to think & that whatever might be Men and Measures, it was my business to be silent & obedient.

(C.L.p.690)

So Burns felt that he had been 'partly forgiven' but that 'all hopes of my getting officially forward are blasted'.

It is my opinion that Burns did not truly realise how serious the complaints were until Corbet arrived from Edinburgh. Surely if he really believed that his Excise post was hanging in the balance he would never have suggested to Robert Graham in the first week of January that he should be considered as officiator for the Galloway district during the absence of McFarlane, the Supervisor. Unfortunately there are no surviving Excise records relating to the Inquiry so the full story will never be known. It is clear, however, from the record of censures and reprimands that Burns was not given an official reprimand nor indeed were his promotion prospects damned. There is no qualifying comment whatsoever against his name on the Excise promotion list. Nevertheless there was no doubt that it had been a close call and I think Burns was now fully aware that he had to behave himself in future. In a letter to George Thomson, the editor of *Select Scottish Airs,* at the end of January, he replied to Thomson's suggestion for a collection of Jacobite songs with a warning 'but would it not give offence'. For Burns to put forward a note of caution shows a changed attitude.

Burns was not a man to be downcast for too long. At the end of January he put forward a proposal to Provost David Staig on how to improve the town's revenues. It concerned the 'town impost' on beer brewed or sold within the Burgh. These town imposts were relics of the days before the Union. As the Excise was then farmed mainly to local tacksmen, many towns were allowed to raise a levy of 2d per barrel, which could be used for specific local purposes. Even after the Union many towns were authorised to continue this local duty. The Dumfries beer duty dated from 1717 and the relevant Act required that the revenue collected should be used to make a harbour, though no doubt over the years it was used for improving other local amenities.

The local duties were completely separate from the Excise duties on beer although the officers were compelled, if required, to provide an ale certificate for all beer produced by their brewers and victuallers, and these certificates formed the basis of the charge to be paid to the local authority. It seems clear from Burns's letter that the Collector was allowed a percentage of the money so collected though there is no evidence in Excise records for this fee.

Burns pointed out to Staig that although the brewers and victuallers in Dumfries paid the local duty, the brewers in Bridgend, just outside the town boundary on the west bank of the Nith, as well as in Annan, paid nothing although most of their beer was sold in Dumfries. Gabriel Richardson, Burns's trader, paid about £30 per annum and he considered that he was in unfair competition with the brewers outside the town. Burns's view was that if a local duty was in force it should be universally assessed and collected. He suggested that Staig should take up the matter with Findlater, who was in a position to instruct all his officers to complete the certificates. The Town Council took up Burns's suggestion.

Just two months later Burns wrote to the Council to apply for his children to be educated at a reduced fee as was his right as Honorary Burgess. Burns reminded the Council of 'his interest on local revenues' and was quick to point out that 'my exertions have secured for you...nearly the sum of ten pounds'. Burns's application was granted and his three sons all attended Dumfries Grammar School.

In May 1793 Burns and his family moved from the very restricting accommodation in the Wee Vennel to a self-contained house in Mill Street, which is now renamed Burns Street. The house was rented at £8 per annum. Robert Junior later described the house;

> [it] was of good order, such as were occupied at that time by the
> better class of burgesses; and my father and mother led a life that
> was comparatively genteel. They also had a maid servant. The
> rooms on the ground floor together with two bedrooms were well
> furnished and carpeted...There was much rough comfort in the
> house, not to be found in those of ordinary citizens.

For the first time, also, Burns had a separate study just off the main bedroom, where he could write and complete his official records in relative peace.

Jean Armour later recalled her husband's domestic life in Dumfries. It would appear that he was not an early riser unless he had an early visit to make to one of his Excise traders. The family breakfasted at 9 o'clock and Burns did most of his Excise work in the morning. They normally dined at 2 o'clock. Mrs. Burns suggested that Burns 'was seldom engaged professionally in the evening'. In this instance perhaps she had suffered a slip of memory because he would have to complete a fair number of evening visits to his traders.

Nevertheless, Mrs. Burns has described a fairly typical Excise officer's life style, which hardly changed for nearly three hundred years and was one of the attractions of the Excise service. Officers invariably worked from home, there were no set hours of work (unlike the Customs) and they were given a large amount of freedom and latitude in how they arranged their day and how they controlled their traders. Other than at the end of every round when Burns was 'employed with my pen until noon–Fine employment for a Poet's pen' (C.L.p.606), and on each collecting day when he was required to attend the Excise Office, his time would be largely his own to organise as he thought fit. Therefore the Excise service was ideally suited to his literary work.

How he managed financially was quite another matter. The £70 salary was certain and quite generous by the standards of the day; though he had to pay for an officiator when he went on private leave. During 1793 and 1794 he made two tours of Galloway with John Syme, his revenue friend. Both were of short duration perhaps because he could ill afford any loss of salary. Also there is no evidence that during his time in Dumfries First Division he was successful in bringing any Excise offences which would have helped to boost his salary. Furthermore, the perquisites Burns had expected from his port duties were never fully realised. He was allowed 6d in the £1 on foreign wine duty up to an annual maximum of £20. In addition he could also receive 8 gallons of proof spirits and 8 lbs. of coffee duty-free each year. Of course, with the outbreak of the French war in February 1793, the import of French wine was strictly prohibited and allied to a general decline in trade Burns's salary suffered as a result. As he pointed out in February 1794, '...some pecuniary share in the ruin of these *****times, losses which, though trifling, were yet what I could not bear.' (C.L.p.469). Indeed twelve months later matters had not improved: 'That part of my salary depended upon the Imports and they are no more for one year' (C.L.p.704). During his whole life he was dogged or worried about money problems. He continually suffered 'the supreme curse of trying to make three guineas do the work of five.'

After his somewhat lucky escape from official censure and his abortive attempt to gain a temporary Supervisor's post, Burns decided, quite wisely, 'to let that matter [the Inquiry] settle before I offer myself too much in the eyes of my Superiors.' (C.L.p.203). And for twelve months he behaved himself and in modern parlance kept a low profile. During this period he no doubt did his work conscientiously and well and there is no mention of the Excise in any of his letters.

Once again Burns walked the political tightrope when, in January 1794, in the midst of a particularly convivial company, he gave the toast, 'may our success in our present war be equal to the justice of the cause.' A certain Captain Dods, who was present, took grave exception to what he considered a revolutionary sentiment and the ensuing squabble almost ended in a duel. Burns, however, was more concerned on how another person present, Samuel Clarke Junior, viewed the matter. Clarke was a Dumfries solicitor who appeared to know William Corbet and some other Head Office officials. Burns quickly wrote two letters to Clarke appealing for his support should the incident be reported back to Corbet or Head Office. He still felt that his character had not been completely cleared; he thought 'some officers there have conceived a prejudice against me as being a drunken dissipated character.' (C.L.p.702). Nothing appeared to·come of the incident but it just showed how concerned Burns had become about his reputation. He really had no cause for alarm because his official character shown in the Register is 'The Poet. Does pretty well', though, of course, Burns would never be aware of that assessment.

In January 1794, almost twelve months to the very day, Burns took up his pen to write once more to Robert Graham. The reason for this letter was to put forward his proposal for improving the Dumfries district;

> ...I have been myself accustommed to labour, & have no notion that
> a servant of the Public should eat the bread of idleness; so, what I
> have long digested, & am going to propose, is the reduction of one
> of our Dumfries Divisions.–Not only in these unlucky times, but
> even in the highest flush of business, my Division, though by far the
> heaviest, was mere trifling.–The others were likely still less.–I
> would plan the reduction as thus.–Let the second Division be
> annihilated; & be divided among the others.–The Duties in it, are,
> two chandlers, a Common Brewer, & some Victuallers; these, with
> some Tea and Spirit Stocks, are the whole Division.–The two
> Chandlers, I would give to the 3d. or Tobacco Division; it is the

RECEIPT FOR SALARY, 1796. *(HMSO)*.

idlest of us all.–That I may seem impartial I will willingly take under my charge, the Common Brewer & the Victuallers.–The Tea & Spirit Stocks, divide between the Bridgend & Dumfries 2d Itinerant Divisions: they have at present but very little, *comparatively*, to do & are quite adequate to the task.–

I assure you, Sir, that, by my plan, the Duties will be equally well charged, & thus an Officer's appointment saved to the Public.–You must remark one thing; that our Common Brewers are, every man of them in Dumfries, completely & unexceptionably, Fair Traders.–One or two, rascally creatures are in the Bridgend Division, but besides being nearly ruined, as all Smugglers deserve, by fines and forfeitures, their business is on the most trifling scale you can fancy–...

(C.L.p.439)

Burns entreated Graham to conceal his identity from Corbet least he thought it 'meddling in his department', and also from Findlater, who was according to Burns, 'not only one of the finest, if not the very first of Excisemen in your Service, but is also one of the worthiest fellows in the universe' (C.L.p.439). Burns, quite rightly, felt that Findlater would be deeply hurt, let alone most annoyed, that Burns had not discussed his plan with him in the first instance.

The poor, unsuspecting officer to lose his post in Burns's proposal was John McQuaker. He had been in the Excise for twenty-two years and during this period had served in no fewer than seven towns (including Mauchline). As Burns mentioned in his postscript, McQuaker was 'burdened with a large family [five children] and many debts'. Poor McQuaker lost his wife a few years later and he died in 1811 still in the Excise at Prestonpans. McQuaker was not highly thought of as an officer, just 'middling good', and indeed he was suspended from duty for three months in May 1796 for an undisclosed offence. This would not justify such callous treatment at the hands of a fellow officer, though McQuaker's application to get his son appointed to the Excise was refused–a sure sign that the Board thought little of the father's abilities.

What were Burns's motives in putting forward such a proposal? If one wished to be charitable one could say that he was purely interested and concerned in the greater efficiency of the Service and the economic use of public monies. That it was done in a most underhand manner cannot be gainsaid, especially as Findlater was a close personal friend. In mitigation it can be said that Burns always operated in this manner, and if he had been challenged his view would have been that there was no point in having a friend or patron in high places unless one used that person. In fairness Burns did recommend McQuaker to Graham's 'humanity and justice'. In the end, of course, the plan came to nothing; indeed it is not known whether Graham even submitted it to Corbet or the Board. When all is said and done, however, the proposal appears to be totally self-centred and it was merely paving the way for his next approach to Graham, which came very soon.

The following month Burns wrote his final letter to Graham. Apparently Burns had heard that Corbet was shortly to become a Collector and that his friend Findlater seemed to be the favourite for Corbet's post (this did actually happen, but not until 1797, a year after Burns's death). How such moves could have benefited Burns is difficult to see until one reads Burns's suggestion to Graham;

> ...Could it be possible then, Sir, that an old Supervisor who may be still be continued, as I know is sometimes the case, after they are rather too infirm for much DUTY, could not such an Officer be appointed to Dumfries, & so let the OFFICIATING JOB fall to my share?–This is a bare possibility, if it be one; so I again beg your pardon for mentioning it, & I have done with the subject.–...
>
> (C.L.p.440)

This was a rather ingenuous if somewhat unscrupulous idea, which of course came to nothing. This proposal shows just how desperate Burns had become to pursue his promotion as the only way to alleviate his financial situation. Indeed, in his last years Burns developed almost an obsession about his money problems, which virtually became a neurosis right up to his death–one of his last letters concerned an outstanding debt. Perhaps also he had at last realised that his health was so deteriorating that there was a grave possibility that it would give up on him before his name came to the top of the list.

Certainly during 1794 he suffered several long bouts of ill-health. The first occurred in January and February when 'he had not been able to lift a pen'. Then in June he wrote from 'a solitary inn' at Castle Douglas, 'I am in poor health ...I am about to suffer for the follies of my youth ..My Medical friends threaten me with flying gout; but I trust that they are mistaken.' (C.L.p.210). Again in September he was 'so poorly as to be scarce able to hold my pen.' The concern now was that the attacks were coming in the summer as well as the winter. At such times Burns could ill-afford to employ an officiator (his salary was halved during sick leave) so he had to struggle as best he could with his full Excise duties, though, as his correspondence tells us, his rheumatic pains were at times excruciating. It is now accepted medical opinion that the rheumatism which attacked him in his early days damaged his heart and thus considerably shortened his life. It is considered that he died from endocarditis. One can only admire his will and determination during the last two years of his life.

At long last, in December 1794, Burns got his chance to officiate as a supervisor during the absence of Findlater on sick leave. As Burns wrote to Mrs. Dunlop to tell her his news;

> ...I look forward to an early period when I shall be appointed in full form: a consummation devoutly to be wished!– My Political sins seem to be forgiven me.–
>
> (C.L.p.213)

The euphoria of getting at least one step, albeit temporary, on the promotion ladder, invested him with a fresh enthusiasm for life; in the New Year his immortal song 'A Man's a man for a that'–'pretty good prose thoughts, inverted into rhyme'–was sent off to Thompson.

If he thought that his new temporary post was one of ease, he was soon to be disabused of such an idea. Several of his letters comment that, 'I have hardly five minutes to myself', or 'a department [supervisorship] that occupies his every hour of the day.' It is fortunate that part of his official diary for the period has survived and from the entries one can get some idea of the hours he worked and an appreciation of the care and attention that he paid to his new responsibilities.

The first entry shows that he visited Sanquhar division, the most northerly of the district, on December 23rd. According to his diary Burns completed a fourteen hour day from 5 o'clock in the morning until 7 o'clock in the evening. During this time he visited no fewer than 12 victuallers, a tanner, a maltster, a chandler and nine tea and tobacco dealers, riding seventeen miles into the bargain. At the victuallers Burns took numerous gauges as well as a 'charge'–dipping the amount brewed to calculate the Excise duty payable. At the tanner he counted 'the depending stock'; this was the tanner's stock of hides and skins, which were dry and ready for sale but were not marked with the Excise seal. Sealing was not normally completed until the skins had already been sold. Supervisors and officers were instructed that such stocks 'should be told over as often as possible, in order to discover whether it be decreased by goods privately taken out.' The officer at Sanquhar was James Graham, who was merely considered 'middling' but on this day his work and books passed Burns's scrutiny as Burns merely added 'Saw nothing in the books meriting report'.

On the following day (Christmas Eve) Burns was up and about early. One can imagine him riding the road to Dumfries before it was light. The next division to visit was his old station–Dumfries First Itinerary–and at eight in the morning he made his first call at Thornhill, where he surveyed two victuallers and a tanner. The day was taken up with an almost complete tour of the area he had controlled just four years earlier, and must have been quite nostalgic for him. Visits to Penpont, Cairnmill, Tynron, Crossford and Dunscore were made before he made his way back to Dumfries and home. During the day he had surveyed twenty traders and by the time he arrived home he had ridden forty miles. Burns had been up and riding for at least sixteen hours and this was Christmas Eve–a formidable workload by any standards especially as he did not arrive in Dumfries until eleven o'clock at night. James Hossacks was the officer in post and he, too, received a clean bill of health from Burns–'nothing to report'. Hossacks had only recently returned to duty after suspension, so that probably accounts for Burns's very close examination of his work. Shortly afterwards Hossacks was moved to Glasgow.

Much closer to home Burns checked the town divisions. His great friend and close neighbour, John Lewars, had moved into Burns's station during his absence and Adam Stobie, a young and inexperienced officer, stood in for Lewars. In both stations Burns surveyed a common brewer and his comments on the two visits were very similar. 'Took off worts at Brewery length as usual'. 'Worts' described the liquor, which was in the process of fermentation, that had been drawn off from the mixture of malt and water. The 'length' was the term used to describe the whole quantity of a single brewing, which the brewer was compelled to declare the quantity to the officer and how much was either 'strong', 'small' or 'tupenny ale'. Both of the visits were undertaken in the evening so on those days Burns was relatively free.

In Dumfries Third Itinerary, which stretched south of Dumfries on the east side of the Nith, Burns experienced for the first time the Excise duty on paper. At Park just outside the town he surveyed a paper-maker. The duty on paper had first been imposed in 1712 and it was a rather complicated trade to understand and control. In those days paper was made mainly from rags and ropes, the better quality writing paper being manufactured from fine rags. There were several classes of paper for duty purposes, each liable at a different rate. Burns merely records that he saw, 'the paper-maker at work, counted depending stock'–like hides, each sheet of paper had to be stamped by the officer.

The only division in which Burns found something at fault was Dumfries First Itinerary, where Leonard Smith was the officer. Smith was, of course, the officer who was moved to give Burns his first Excise post. Since then he had been suspended from duty and on his recall he spent his time in various Dumfries divisions covering for officers on leave. When checking a maltster, Burns found that Smith had made some trifling errors during his last survey and then on examining his books he found 'several other instances of a like nature,' Nevertheless, there is no evidence that Smith, on this occasion, received any reprimand for the errors, though Burns's diary was examined and initialled by Mitchell.

It is certainly very clear from this valuable Excise record that Burns acted as supervisor in a most able and capable manner. He obviously worked most conscientiously and nothing seemed to miss his eagle eye. There seems no doubt from this evidence that he was quite capable of taking up a full-time post at the higher grade. Whether he felt the extra £12 or so salary he received was worth the extra work and the long hours of travelling is rather debatable.

Burns spent about four months officiating and Findlater returned to duty towards the middle of April 1795. Even after he was back at his old station, Burns found himself answering enquiries from Head Office. In April he wrote to John Edgar, who was the Accountant to the Excise Board. Burns had heard (possibly from Mitchell) that he was going to be censured for not sending in the Wine Account for the district. Burns felt that he needed to explain the situation. It would appear that once he had received the order from Edinburgh for the account, he immediately checked the wine stocks of as many officers as he could and asked the outlying officers to send their books to him. At about this time Findlater returned to duty and Burns assumed that he would now deal with the matter. The one officer who had not complied with Burns's instruction was James Graham of Sanquhar.

It appears to be a rather minor transgression and one caused by handing over duties to Findlater. Burns, ever conscious of his reputation at Head Office, ended his letter;

> ...if I must still be thought censurable, I hope it will be considered,
> that this Officiating Job being my first, I cannot be supposed to be
> completely master of all the etiquette of the business.–...
>
> (C.L.p.718)

His private thoughts on the supervisor's job he expressed to Patrick Heron, the Whig candidate who had asked Burns for some help in his election campaign. It also seems from Burns's letter that Heron had suggested that he might be able to help Burns's Excise career if elected.

Burns kindly thanked him for his interest but then explained in most polite terms that Heron would be powerless to help;

> ...The statement is this–I am on the supervisor's list, and as we
> come on there by precedency, in two or three years I shall be at the
> head of that list, and be appointed, *of course. Then* a FRIEND might
> be of service to me in getting me into a place of the kingdom which I

would like. A supervisor's income varies from about a hundred and twenty, to two hundred a year; but the business is incessant drudgery, and would be near a compleat bar to every species of literary pursuit. The moment I am appointed supervisor, in the common routine, I may be nominated on the collector's list; and this is always a business purely of political patronage. A collectorship varies much, from better than two hundred a year to near a thousand. They also come forward by precedency on the list; and have besides a handsome income, a life of compleat leisure. A life of literary leisure with a decent competence, is the summit of my wishes...

(C.L.p.715)

Within a few months of acknowledging that Heron's interest was of little use to him at the present, Burns found himself explaining the system of patronage to Maria Riddell. She had asked *his* advice on behalf of a protegé of hers. Burns explained that the Excise was 'a superior object' to the Customs. If the candidate had more than three children, however, he could not be accepted into the Excise. The best plan was to find out whether any of her friends had a contact with one of the Excise Commissioners and then try to interest them, though he wisely added 'the more the better'! As he pointed out the Commissioners of both Boards 'are people in the fashionable circle & must be known to many of your friends'. It must have been a strange experience for Burns to be sought out for his knowledge and experience so far as patronage was concerned.

With the highpoint of his Excise career over, the remainder of the year brought Burns little joy but much pain and unhappiness. In the summer he suffered another bout of ill-health and in September Elizabeth Riddell, his only legitimate daughter, died at the age of three after a long and harrowing illness. She was buried at Mauchline and Burns was unable to attend the funeral 'to pay his last duties to her'. He was distraught at her death;

...I have lately drank deep of the cup of affliction...

(C.L.p.215)

During the year he had also lost the pleasure and comfort of his constant correspondent Mrs. Dunlop; she had taken deep offence at certain remarks he made about French Royalists. Mrs. Dunlop ignored 'two packets' of his letters and they were only reconciled on his deathbed.

There is no evidence that either his enthusiasm or his ability was diminished, nor indeed that he sank into drunkenness. In January he had been instrumental in forming the Dumfries Volunteers and for most of the year he took an active part in all the business connected with the Corps. Indeed he was one of the eight members of the governing committee. He was also active in selecting books for the newly established Dumfries library. His literary work continued apace and, until the last months of the year, Burns continued to undertake his full Excise duties. Findlater later recorded, 'It was not till the latter ends of his days that there was any falling off in respect of his attention to business and this was amply accounted for in the presence of disease and accumulating infirmities.' During October he was confined to his house and in December he suffered a most severe bout of fever, which in his words, 'brought me to the borders of the grave.'

SCRAP OF A NOTE-BOOK IN BURNS' HANDWRITING WHEN ACTING
AS SUPERVISOR. (HMSO).

(C.L.p.279). With his health so obviously deteriorating and beset with problems it is quite amazing that Burns managed to continue his Excise work, let alone maintain his literary output.

Ever present during this period were his financial worries–real or otherwise. In December he wrote to Mrs. Dunlop, 'If I am cut off, even in all the vigour of manhood as I am, gracious God, what will become of my little flock..' (C.L.p.213). Indeed, at his death Burns owed only ten pounds and to balance that there was something more than two hundred pounds owing to his estate. On 'Hogmanai eve 1795' he was forced to send round to Mitchell, his Collector, a request for an advance of one guinea out of his next round's salary; the sums were paid eight times a year at the end of each collecting round–in arrears of course! Such a request was not unusual in either the Customs or Excise services. Burns, however, felt the need to enclose with the advance application (not a loan as many biographers have suggested) a poem dedicated to Mitchell, 'Friend of the Poet, tried and leal...' (C.W.p.561), which, considering his situation, contained such optimistic lines that he still had a share of health and the promise of more life. Unfortunately time was not on his side.

It was normal Excise procedure that when an officer was on sick leave his salary was halved, the difference being paid to the officer who officiated in his post. So Burns would only be entitled to £35 rather than his full £70. Robert Chambers, who published a life of Burns in 1851-52, maintained that Adam Stobie, the young officer who officiated for Burns, refused to accept one penny piece extra and thus Burns retained his full salary until the day of his death. Unfortunately this story is not borne out by either the Excise records or indeed by Burns himself.

On 7th July 1796 Burns wrote to Alexander Cunningham;

> ...What way, in the name of thrift, shall I maintain myself & keep a horse in Country-quarters–with a wife & five children at home on 35£? I mention this, because I had intended to beg your utmost interest & all friends you can muster to move our Commissioners of Excise to grant me the full salary.–I dare say you know them all personally...
>
> (C.L.p.473)

And just five days later he wrote again, '...my plan is to address the Board by petition and then if any friend has thrown in his word 'tis a great deal in my favour.'

The Excise record, now in the Scottish Record Office, shows the discharge of Burns's salary during the last five months. On 3rd March he received £6, on 14th April £3, 2nd June £6 again and a final payment of £2 on 14th July just one week before he died. The rapid and sudden collapse of his health is tragically recorded in this document, the firm and bold signature in March and April so deteriorated that by July it is almost unrecognisable. Indeed if further evidence is needed, Findlater stated that Burns wrote to Robert Graham in the hope that he would use his influence to get his full salary during his sickness. Graham, however, was unable to comply with Burns's request but 'sent him a private donation of £5, which I believe nearly or totally compensated the loss.' Dr. Currie, Burns's first biographer, suggests that Graham's 'offer of assistance' was contained in a letter dated 11th July 1796.

The last month of Burns's life is well-known. From 3rd July to 16th July he was at Brow Well near Ruthwell on the Solway Firth, where it was hoped that sea-bathing and the mineral waters of the district would restore his health. It was here that he met Maria Riddell for the last time. She later recorded, 'The stamp of death was imprinted on his features' and that his first greeting to her was, 'Well Madam, have you any commands for the other world?' She remained his most constant supporter after his death and wrote a most fair and generous sketch of him for the *Dumfries Weekly Journal* in August 1796.

Burns returned to Dumfries on 18th July and could barely walk from the carriage to the door of his house. For the last few days of his life he was nursed by Jessie Lewars, John's sister, because his wife was expecting their ninth child, a son who was born on the day of Burns's funeral. John Syme, his close friend, saw him on the 19th and believed 'it is all over with him...the hand of Death is visibly fixed upon him.' On 21st July Syme wrote to Alexander Cunningham with the sad news, 'Burns departed this morning at 5 o'clock'. Four days later Burns was buried in St. Michael's churchyard with full military honours. It was reported that over ten thousand persons joined in the funeral procession. Then, far away in Edinburgh, some unknown Excise clerk entered 'Dead' in the Examiner's Register; the short but eventful career of the most illustrious Excise officer had come to an end.

Almost as soon as Burns was laid to rest the vilification of his character started. The obituary notices first set the trend. The *Edinburgh Advertiser* wrote that 'his extraordinary endowments were accompanied with frailties which rendered them useless to himself and his family'; and the *Scots Magazine* said much the same thing. One must lay most blame with his first biographers. Robert Heron, an acquaintance of Burns from Edinburgh days, published his memoir of the poet in March 1797. Although he credited the young Burns with some virtues, he portrayed his life from 1787 to 1796 as one of unrelieved blackness: 'He sank, by degrees, into the boon companion of mere excisemen, and almost every drunken fellow, who was willing to spend his money lavishly in the alehouse, could easily command the company of Burns.' One wonders what Messrs Mitchell, Findlater and Lewars thought of the derogatory tone of 'mere excisemen'? This travesty of the truth was even reprinted in 1834 when other persons, who knew Burns intimately during these years, had countered such views.

The most influential and damaging biography, however, was that by Dr. James Currie published in 1800. This left the reader in no doubt that Burns, during the later years of his life, was an alcoholic, who had drunk himself into an early grave. Unfortunately Currie's work enjoyed immense success and in twenty years scores of editions were published, until the tradition of Burns's debauchery and drunkenness had been firmly established. Irving, writing eight years later in his *Lives of the Scottish poets,* suggested that Burns 'showed lamentable deviations from the sober parts of life and had almost degraded to a level with the outcasts of society'. Most later writers accepted Currie's views but also vied with each other to blacken Burns's character further. Josiah Walker, who had met Burns briefly in Dumfries, wrote a critical memoir of Burns in 1811, which only added fuel to the tradition. At the time Walker was Collector of Customs at Perth. Even Sir Walter Scott took part in the debate, and in his review of one of the biographies he implied that Burns was actually a good deal worse than Currie had made out!

The first writer to attempt to correct the balance was Alexander Peterkin in 1818, when he issued a reprint of Currie's edition of Burns's works with an added preface. It is in this edition that Peterkin included Findlater's testimony:

> My connexion with Robert Burns commenced immediately after his admission into the Excise and continued to the hour of his death. In all that time the superintendance of his behaviour as an officer of the revenue was a branch of my especial providence, and as it may be supposed, I would not be inattentive observer of the general conduct of a man and a poet so celebrated by his countrymen...he was exemplary in his attention as an Excise-officer and was even jealous of the least imputation on his vigilance...and I will further avow, that I never saw him, which was very frequently while he lived in Ellisland and still more so, almost every day after he removed to Dumfries, but in the hours of business he was quite himself, and capable of discharging the duties of his office; nor was he ever known to drink by himself or seen to indulge in the use of liquor in the forenoon, as the statement that he was perpetually under the stimulus, unequivocally implies.

> ...I have seen Burns in all his various phases–in his convivial moments, in his sober moods and in the bosom of his family; indeed I believe I saw more of him than any other individual had occasion to see him, after he became an Exciseman; and I never beheld anything like the gross enormities with which he is now charged...the virulence indeed with which his memory has been treated is hardly to be paralleled in the annals of literature.

One would have thought that such an outright rebuttal of all the defamatory comments on Burns by a person best qualified to know the true position, would have settled the matter once and for all; but yet they were still being repeated into the present century. To make matters worse in the next twenty years both Lockhart and Allan Cunningham wrote biographies of Burns, which put forward so many misleading and inaccurate stories about Burns that continued to be repeated for almost one hundred years. It was not until the 1930s that the first fair, balanced and true portraits of Burns were published and then his achievements and character were properly vindicated. It is, perhaps, coincidental that the most famous of these works were all by foreign writers!–Professor Snyder, Hans Hecht and Catherine Carswell.

The mistaken notion that Burns's career as an Excise officer was marred by irregular conduct was first refuted in 1895 by John Sinton, an Excise Supervisor at Carlisle, in a paper read to the local Burns's club. Such was its importance and relevance to the study of the poet during the run-up to the centennial celebrations of his death that Sinton decided to publish a small volume at his own expense. The slim book, entitled *Burns: Excise Officer and Poet, a vindication,* was an immediate success and in a couple of years had run into four editions. The fourth or 'Jubilee' edition, published in 1897, had a foreword by Lord Rosebery, who was then Honourary President of the Burns Federation, and contained extracts of

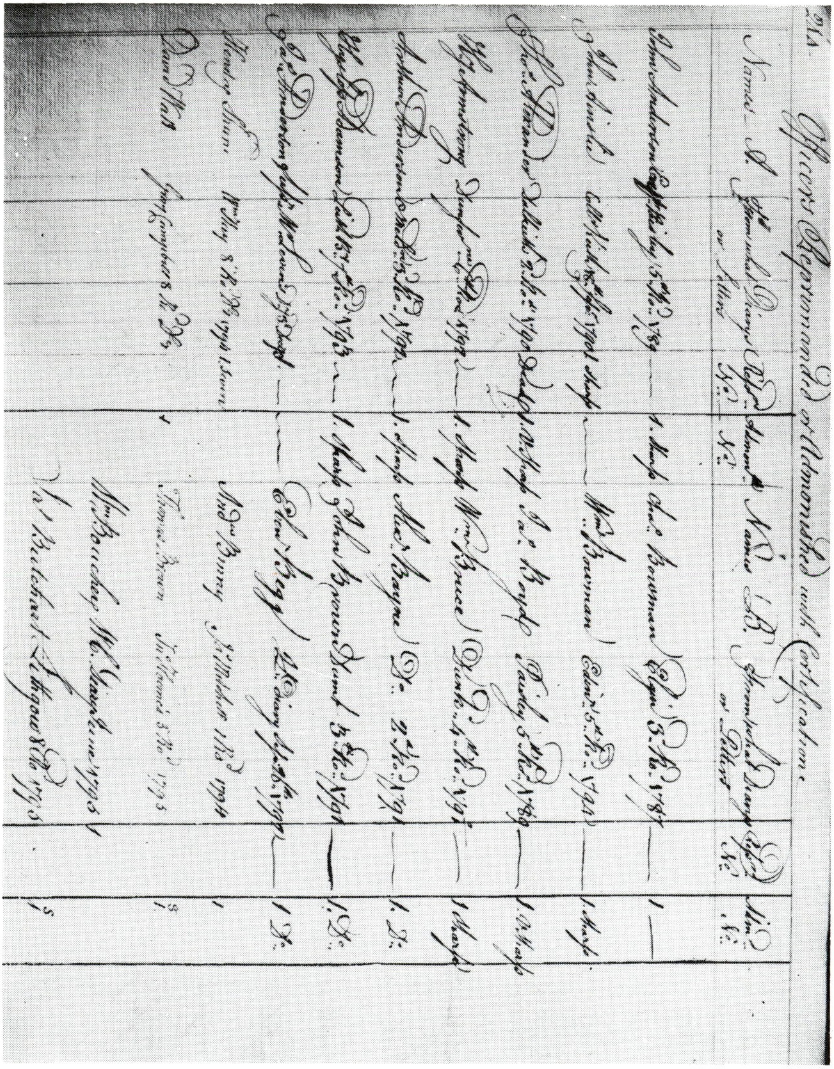

EXCISE HEAD OFFICE REGISTER OF OFFICERS REPRIMANDED. *(HMSO).*

his address on the centenary of the poet's death. It is amazing to read comments such as 'the weaknesses of men like Burns', 'lapses and catastrophes' and 'great in gifts and great in temptation; great in strength and great in weakness' The tradition still lived!

Sinton based his paper and subsequent book mainly on records 'carefully extracted from the original registers of the Scottish Excise Board'. These registers had been found in the Excise headquarters in London in 1857 by an observant Inspector named James Macfadzean. The discovery of the volumes was most fortuitous; Macfadzean had been given the task of looking through a miscellaneous collection of books prior to their destruction. Luckily he realised the importance of the information on Burns and he obtained the Excise Secretary's permission to make copies. Macfadzean later became the Collector at Glasgow and his son Robert, who was his Chief Clerk, transcribed the copies in 1892 for Sinton's use. Macfadzean used the material himself as the basis of several articles for the *Burns Chronicle,* which was first published in 1891.

The documents enabled Sinton to prove categorically that not only was Burns held in high esteem by the Scottish Excise Board but that he was never once censured. He could also confirm that Burns's name was never removed from the Examiners' promotion list. Sinton's book was of inestimable value in countering most of the incorrect and malicious stories of Burns's Excise career. Sinton completed what Findlater had attempted to do some eighty years earlier–a complete and full vindication of Burns's reputation as an Excise officer. The Grand Old Man of Politics, William Gladstone, on reading the book in 1895, expressed the view, 'The loyalty of the Excise to the Poet is very remarkable and does credit to both.'

In only one respect was Sinton wrong. He stated that the Registers 'have disappeared but the extracts remain..' Fortunately some of the registers did survive and they are now proudly held by Her Majesty's Customs and Excise with the kind permission of the Scottish Record Office. Another thirty years were to pass before other misconceptions about Burns's Excise career were finally cleared. Fergusons monumental edition of Burns's letters threw a new light on what Burns, himself, felt and thought about his profession. Then the discovery of Crawfurd's diary a few years later provided a new insight into the *Rosamond* smuggling affair.

During his Excise career Burns had wisely paid 6s (30p) a quarter to the 'Excise Incorporation'–virtually a Widows' and Orphans' Fund. The entry in the account for 1796 shows against Burns's name 'Died 21st July 1796 & left a Widow and children'. In 1797 there is the first reference of a payment to Jean Armour. It amounted to £8 per annum and this pension continued until 1821 when it was increased to £12. Burns's widow continued to receive this annuity until her death in 1834. Burns's total contributions during his career were just under £10, yet his widow received a total of £365. Although we know Burns 'does pretty well' it may be said that Jean Armour 'did rather better'.

There is not a shadow of doubt that Burns was a very efficient and effective Excise officer; even the most able officers received reprimands or censures at some time during their careers but Burns's record remained unblemished. That he was of above average ability has been confirmed by Findlater and had he survived, Burns would surely have ended his Excise career as a collector, a post of relative ease and financial comfort that he had merely dreamed about–'A life of literary leisure with a handsome competency'. Such a post would have been his just reward. The suggestion that his post was a sinecure has, I hope, been amply disproved.

During his short Excise career Burns managed to transcend the laborious and monotonous nature of the work; he patiently suffered the pettifogging and annoying aspects of Excise minutiae; he survived the physical rigours of Excise life and withstood the unpopularity of his chosen profession–all no mean achievements for a man of his constitution, character, passion and pride. From being a most unlikely candidate for service in the revenue Burns became a dedicated, conscientious and admirable Excise officer–a positive credit to the Scottish Excise service.

Her Majesty's Customs and Excise has always taken an immense pride in its most illustrious Excise officer and has been most loyal to his immortal memory. Burns merely hoped that his profession would take credit from him and this it has done for almost two hundred years. The 'poor, damn'd, rascally Gager' has passed into the folklore of the Department and he fully justifies his position of pre-eminence amongst such literary giants as Chaucer, Dryden, Congreve, Paine and Adam Smith.